PHOTOS BY RETO GUNTLI · TEXT BY SUNIL SETHI
ED. ANGELIKA TASCHEN

INSIDE ASIA

TASCHEN

HONG KONG KÖLN LONDON LOS ANGELES MADRID PARIS TOKYO

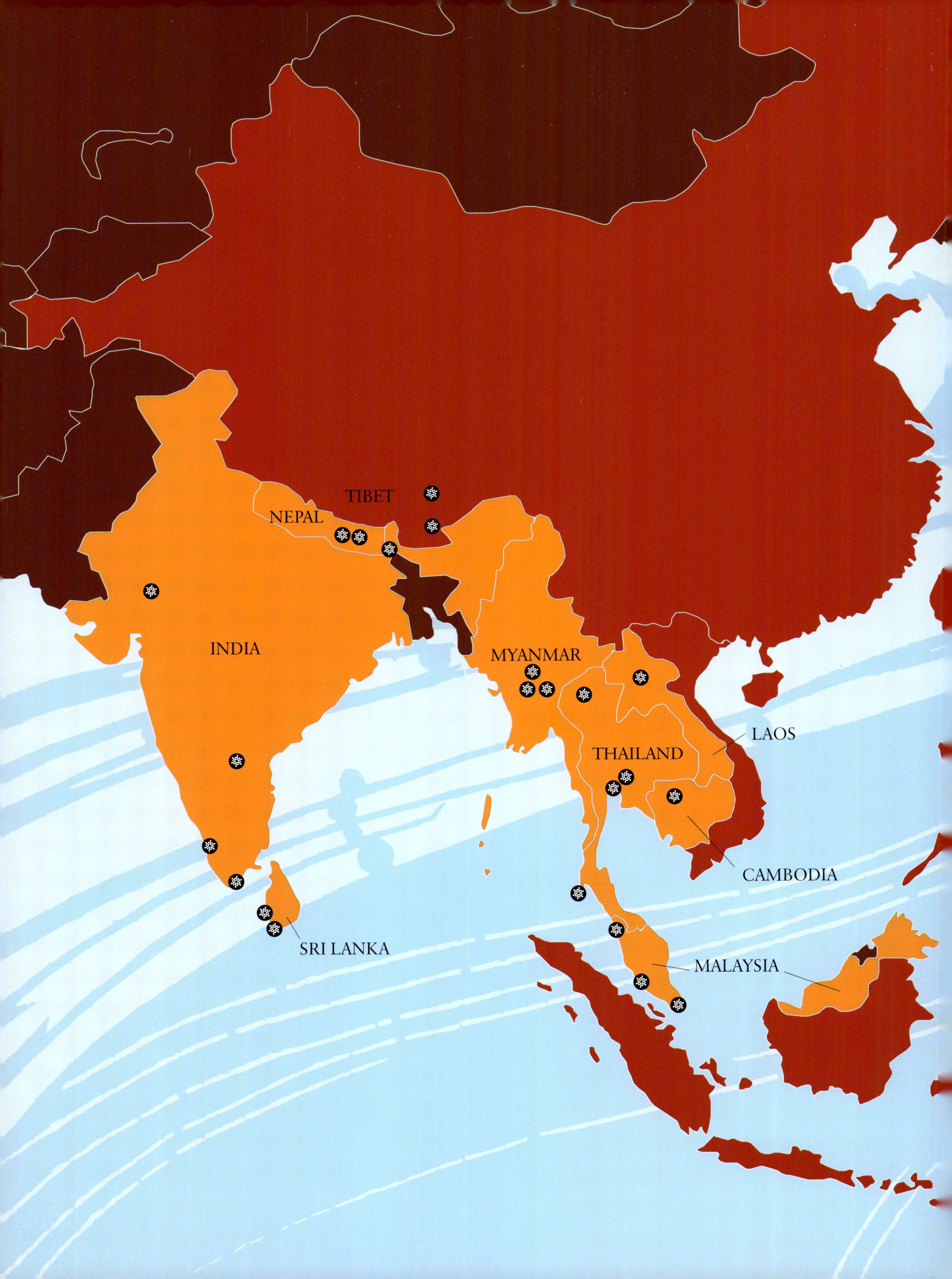

TIBET
NEPAL
INDIA
MYANMAR
LAOS
THAILAND
CAMBODIA
SRI LANKA
MALAYSIA

Going with the Flow: A Journey into the Heart of Asia

by Reto Guntli

Asia has played a significant role throughout most of my adult life. A genuine passion for the exotic continent and its people, and the interest in Eastern philosophy and mysticism persuaded me to spend a few years there in my early twenties. The relationship has been kept fresh and alive by countless visits since then. When Angelika Taschen approached me with the book project "Eastern Interiors" while working on her "The Hotel Book. Great Escapes Asia", I loved the idea and accepted with great enthusiasm.

In April 2003 I left for Delhi to meet Sunil Sethi, the intended author for this book project, to discuss our collaboration. A visit to the Taj Mahal turned into a nightmare that was to change the course of events. A devastating car accident left me seriously injured on the road. The agonizing rescue mission and airlift back to Zurich for the operation of a broken cervical vertebra saved my life. During the months of recovery at home and time for contemplation, I decided to view life at its face value and make the best of it. By focusing on the improvements of every single day, the future took on a whole new meaning. It was a second chance at life and I was grateful for it. It took this painful experience to think about life's truths. From the perspective that every day should be graciously appreciated, a new life-force seemed to take hold. Accepting a world where nothing is to be taken for granted opened doors to unexpected possibilities and joys.

Three months later – the day I took off my neck brace – I was on the plane to Bali. The exotic isle had become my secret getaway ever since I lived there at the age of nineteen. A high-spirited time of great freedom had left a lasting impact on my years ahead. In the back of my mind I have always tried to preserve that light-hearted spirit anywhere I went. All of us travellers discovering Bali in the late seventies wanted to live there forever, we were seduced by the lush tropical nature and the charm of its warm and gentle people. Some of us made Bali their home, like Anita Lococo, whose lasting friendship kept the memories alive. Today she rents out tropical holiday homes to travellers and rock stars. Bali is a showcase of some of the most innovative architecture and design of Asia, and Anita and I made sure I had a good start. To this day, a profound spirituality is expressed in the Balinese alluring and mysterious rituals. Every-day life, religion and nature are one interdependent entity in their cosmos. With depth, sincerity and a sense of humour they face their challenges very gracefully. Much can be learned from their simple and truthful ways. Values that would be applicable in the bigger picture – anywhere.

When Angelika viewed the first photo reportages from Bali in Berlin, she realized that since Buddhist values like harmony and serenity found their way into people's rural and urban homes, Buddhism would have to become the red line in the book. Thanks to her own attraction to and fascination with Eastern cultures and spirituality, Angelika proceeded to edit the photos with great insight while the photo material poured in from all over Asia.

From the coffee plantation in Java to historic quarters in Malaysia, private islands in the Philippines or even suburban homes in Manila and Singapore, organic materials, Buddhist art and meditative Zen spaces showed the need for a contemplative, authentic and even spiritual approach to home living.

My glamorous friend Kathy de Guzman, socialite and world traveller, showed me around her native Philippines for a glance into the lifestyles of the most hospitable people. We went island hopping, walked on the whitest beaches on earth and danced to Latin music. The extraverted, fun-loving ways of the Philippinos have a very South American feel. When we moved on to Singapore to meet Kathy's "fish-bowl" of star architects and designer friends, the highly prosperous model state of Asia showed stunning sophistication. Their contemporary homes reflect the search for tranquillity through the means of clean, minimalist lines and spaces, creating islands of peace in a bustling, modern city.

A short flight in Asia is often like a journey back in time. Myanmar is poor and backward, lacking the development of its neighbouring countries. But it is breathtakingly beautiful and has a stunning Buddhist heritage. Visitors are welcome in their monasteries and pagodas. In fact, nowhere in Asia was I ever turned away at a door to a Buddhist sight. Myanmar is still unspoiled, authentic and the Burmese are affectionate, shy, but curious. In charming ways they show their delight about people visiting their country from so far away. Like often in Asia, much respect and attention is dedicated to us foreigners. There is a refreshing innocence about the people of Myanmar, hardly ever encountered elsewhere.

By February 2004, the photo material had become so vast and diverse that a two-volume "Inside Asia" was to replace the originally planned "Eastern Interiors" in only one volume. It meant a much greater challenge of going beyond private interiors and style. It was to include the "Sangha", the order of the Buddhist monks and nuns, as well as the greatest Buddhist monuments. With great drive and raring to go, I faced twice the amount of work and the same deadline. Asian massage and acupuncture techniques helped soothe and eventually cure my pain in the neck. Paired with lots of swimming, yoga and a focused mind, it was the best therapy. Rather than sit over endless preparations, I trusted my intuitions, followed a gut feeling and the next day I was on the plane: in total 67 flights in seven months. Spontaneously going with the flow proved to be the right choice; unrestricted curiosity and considerable good luck would provide the rest. This attitude took me to places I had never even imagined.

The plane from Luang Prabang was cancelled several times as rice fields were burning all over Laos. Smoke painted the city and landscape in a yellow, surreal glow. With the blessing of the highly revered Grand Satou, head of the Laotian Buddhists, I was able to partake in the disciplined, graceful lives of monks and novices at the revered temples and monasteries of Laos. Architects working for the Unesco showed me the outstanding architectural planning of the formal royal city, a jewel built inside a loop of the Mekong River. It is a place where clocks have stopped ticking and the nostalgia of Indochina lingers on.

In Cambodia, I pulled Kathy up the temple ruin of Angkor Wat to staggering heights. Vertigo was terrifying her, but I insisted she had to face and overcome her fear. She had the opportunity of climbing the most mysterious and impressive monument made by man. Reaching the top and viewing the vast sacred city, dedicated entirely to spiritual life, was indeed a superb emotion well worth Kathy's effort. The grand-scaled ruins are immersed in a jungle where trees and roots exuberantly grow over Hindu and Buddhist temples and giant sculptures. The perfect artworks represent the divine – frozen in stone – to outlast time. How a place of such grandeur, a civilization of such superior cultural skill and wisdom, could simply disappear and be forgotten for six hundred years remains a mystery. We explored the immense temple area in an American jeep from the period here called the "American War". Having been captured by the Vietcong, recaptured by the Khmer Rouge and then by Cambodian troops, this country has had to suffer a cruel recent history to which the vehicle we drove was a witness. The trauma is still there, as even children have heartbreaking stories to tell. But there is much hope in the people and their strong will to move ahead to a new future. The Cambodians are relearning their crafts, reviving their arts and hoping for tourism to help develop the country. The jeep now belongs to the Amansara Resort.

Hanoi's oldest temple is a small island rising from the mist of a lake. Novices in dark-brown robes opened the gates to spacious courtyards. In Hué, Mr. Ahn's home was built according to Feng Shui principles by a Princess whose painting is revered in the family shrine. Balanced harmony is believed to have much to do with the elements surrounding us, especially wind and water. Good energies have to flow, bad ones are kept out – an atmosphere of peace is created by the flow of "chi", the energy surrounding us. At his humble house inside the citadel, the cousin to the last Emperor Baudai pulled out his court robes from a box underneath his bed. The old man showed me to the "Forbidden Purple City", where he had spent his entire childhood. Inside the few buildings that have survived American bombs, those who knew him bowed briefly, while others were amused by the man in shabby silks. As he recalled life at court with shiny eyes, remembering secret doors and passages, it struck me that the fate of "The Last Emperor" of China could not have been much different.

Meanwhile, Sunil Sethi was facing a different situation in Japan where he spent many weeks on preparations. In a country where entertaining at home is not part of the etiquette, receiving a "gaijin" (Japanese for foreigner) photographer was unheard of. At the peak of Japan's economic miracle in 1980 I had spent 18 months in Tokyo and am no stranger to the complexities of Japanese society. A history of isolation has made Japan a culture apart and I was not surprised to find attitudes and lifestyles virtually unchanged after my long absence. The majority of people in the richest and most advanced nation in Asia live in concrete cubicle homes in endless, neon-lit suburbs. A ride from Tokyo to Osaka on the "Shinkansen" train is a sad tribute to the alarming absence of urban planning, the reckless destruction of traditional infrastructure and the loss of nature. One generation's obsession with progress and the rising economy have completely changed the landscape of the country. Today, the people of Japan are starting to realize what price they have paid. Most concerned about preserving Japanese heritage is American writer Alex Kerr. His traditional homes at a Shinto shrine near Kyoto and an old farmhouse in the forgotten Iya valley are rare examples of the sense of aesthetics that used to be inherent in Japan's every-day life. Fortunately, these aesthetics are incorporated in the radical architecture of genius architects like Tadao Ando or Kengo Kuma who bring "Zen" into materials as crude as concrete.

China amazed me with a vibrant, dynamic edge. From a country I perceived as gloomy and poor twenty years ago, a new China had arisen. The recent boom to a superpower of productivity has made a huge impact on the lives of many Chinese. "Enrich yourselves", Confucius once lectured and the Communist Party of the People's Republic wisely passed on the message to the people. Nearly half a billion Chinese have overcome poverty. World economists pray for a stable China while everyone wants to get a piece of the pie in the latest "Eldorado" (gold rush). While staying at the posh China Club in Beijing, Giorgio Armani, Dick Cheney and Condoleezza Rice made their appearance, and Anthony Minghella celebrated the première of his film "Cold Mountain" there, accompanied by Renée Zellweger. Two thousand high-rises were built in Shanghai in the past decade. The "Bund" in the former English Concession has become a boulevard of western luxury and sophistication. Alongside a part of the Great Wall, architects have created the "Commune by the Great Wall", a project with the ambition to put China on the map of international architecture and design. "Made in China" has gone global. The homes of European expatriates, however, pay tribute to an ancient culture in a nostalgic celebration of imperial China.

Karma, my Himalayan guide, took me to the inner sanctums of Tibet's sacred places. Entering the dark and smoky atmosphere of this inner realm of Tibetan Buddhism is a deeply mysterious and moving experience. Old and young pilgrims, villagers and nomads stream into Lhasa on the back of trucks, by foot or prostrate over hundreds of miles. The hardship of life in Himalayan altitudes, where everything has the clout of mystery, drama and meaning, is deeply engraved in the weathered, friendly faces. Their eyes light up and shine with deepest devotion in the face of highly revered Buddhas, guarded by gods and demons. Karma talked of many secrets and legends of Tibet, where Buddhism has permeated life for over a thousand years. It is a place where phenomena like the slightest change of wind or a strange formation of a cloud bear metaphysical significance. In Tantric Buddhism, esoteric rituals and meditation are deeply associated. Rituals and music are being performed in renovated temples and the monasteries are increasingly filling with eager scholars. Karma invited me to his prayers to Jobo, Tibet's most sacred Buddha idol inside the Jokhang temple. Lining up with the pilgrims to receive the blessings, I wished for a rainbow. Later that day at the Dalai Lama's Summer Palace, a sudden sandstorm darkened the blue sky, followed by a thunderstorm. Taking refuge at the hotel, I climbed to the roof and saw the beautiful rainbow over old Lhasa. Karma interpreted this as a sign of great fortune. As light is the key to photography, this incident carried great symbolism.

I visited India again and drove in a car, maybe with the intention of confronting demons that might still have been lingering in my mind since my accident. But I couldn't find them, they were gone: no pain, no blame, no regret, no nightmares. I had accepted the fate, learned its lesson and moved on to what became one of the best years in my life. I found a feeling of liberation, even peace, in that.

Positive attitude matters - most Asians would agree – and it held in store many magic moments with old and new friends and countless heart-warming experiences at the most unexpected places. "Inside Asia" also had a very positive impact on the professionals working on the book. Agi Simões, who has been working with me for eight years, was of great assistance on the project. He has now found the confidence to challenge his own photography career. For Angelika, the editing of her "firework book" became like a meditative act in which she withdrew from any outside influences, she later told me. Everyone was strangely affected by the good karma the book obviously embraced.

"Inside Asia" does not claim to be a book about Buddhism. Buddhism is not tied to localities, it resides in men's hearts. It is rather a journey to places of great beauty and harmony, where Buddha is revered and where Buddhist wisdom and philosophy have penetrated people's private homes and lives.

To reflect the intensity and authenticity of the varied atmospheres of living spaces in Asia, I photographed "Inside Asia" entirely in daylight which means available light on conventional film. The contents and the moods of the photos remain accurate, as no retouching or digital corrections have been made.

Going with the Flow: Eine Reise in das Herz Asiens

von Reto Guntli

Seit ich erwachsen bin, spielt Asien eine große Rolle in meinem Leben. Meine Leidenschaft für diesen exotischen Kontinent und seine Menschen, für östliche Philosophie und Mystik führten mich mit Anfang zwanzig für einige Jahre dorthin. Seitdem fahre ich regelmäßig nach Asien. Als Angelika Taschen mit dem Buchprojekt »Eastern Interiors« an mich herantrat, während ich gerade für ihr »The Hotel Book. Great Escapes Asia« fotografierte, nahm ich begeistert an.

In April 2003 flog ich zu einem ersten Treffen mit Sunil Sethi, dem Autor des Buches, nach Delhi. Wir wollten uns dem Projekt gemeinsam annähern, aber nach einem Ausflug zum Taj Mahal war nichts mehr wie zuvor. Nach einem Grauen erregenden Autounfall blieb ich schwer verletzt auf der Straße zurück. Die qualvolle Rettungsaktion und der anschließende Krankentransport nach Zürich, wo mein gebrochener Halswirbel operiert wurde, retteten mir das Leben. Während der langen Rekonvaleszenz zu Hause kam ich nach langem Nachdenken zu dem Schluss, das Leben so zu nehmen, wie es war. Indem ich mich auf die Fortschritte jedes einzelnen Tages konzentrierte, bekam das Wort Zukunft eine völlig neue Bedeutung für mich. Dankbar erkannte ich, dass das Leben mir eine zweite Chance gegeben hatte, und nahm diese Erfahrung zum Anlass, über die Wahrheiten des Daseins nachzudenken. Aus der Haltung, dass man jeden neuen Tag dankbar begrüßen sollte, schöpfte ich Kraft und Lebensfreude. Wenn man in der Welt nichts mehr für gegeben hält, eröffnen sich unerwartete Möglichkeiten und Freuden.

Drei Monate später – an dem Tag, an dem meine Halsstütze abgenommen wurde – war ich auf dem Flug nach Bali. Seit ich mit neunzehn dort gelebt hatte, war diese exotische Insel meine geheime Zuflucht geblieben. Die lebhafte Erfahrung großer Freiheit hat mich geprägt. Insgeheim habe ich mich bemüht, mir diese unbeschwerte Fröhlichkeit zu erhalten, wo immer ich war. Wir alle, die wir Bali in den späten 1970er Jahren für uns entdeckten, wollten für immer dort bleiben, so sehr hatten uns die üppige tropische Natur und der Charme der warmherzigen Menschen verzaubert. Einige der damaligen Reisegefährten wie Anita Lococo zogen tatsächlich nach Bali, und unsere tiefe Freundschaft hielt die Erinnerung lebendig. Inzwischen vermietet sie in den Tropen Ferienhäuser an Touristen und Rockstars. Bali ist ein Schaufenster für das kreative Design Asiens, und für Anita und mich wurde es zu einem guten Startpunkt der Reise. Bis heute drücken die verführerischen, geheimnisvollen Rituale der Balinesen tiefe Spiritualität aus. Religion, Natur und Alltag sind in ihrem Kosmos untrennbar miteinander verbunden – charakterstark, ernsthaft und anmutig stellen die Balinesen sich mit einem feinen Sinn für Humor den Herausforderungen des Lebens. Von ihrer einfachen wahrhaftigen Art kann man nur lernen – Werte von im Grunde allgemeiner Gültigkeit.

Als Angelika in Berlin die ersten Fotoreportagen aus Bali sichtete, sah sie, dass die Häuser auf dem Land wie auch in der Stadt buddhistische Wertvorstellungen wie Harmonie und Gelassenheit widerspiegeln. Buddhismus sollte der rote Faden des Buches werden. Da sie sich selbst zu östlichen Kulturen und ihrer Spiritualität hingezogen fühlt, editierte Angelika das Fotomaterial, das aus ganz Asien bei ihr eintraf, mit großem Feingefühl.

Von der Kaffeeplantage in Java über die historischen Wohnviertel in Malaysia, Privatinseln auf den Philippinen bis zu Häusern am Stadtrand von Singapur: Überall spiegeln organische Baumaterialien, buddhistische Kunst und meditative Zen-Räume das Bedürfnis nach einem kontemplativen, authentischen, ja spirituellen Verständnis des Lebens zu Hause.

Meine mondäne Freundin Kathy de Guzman, Weltreisende und Angehörige der Schickeria, bot mir in ihrem Heimatland, den Philippinen, einen Blick auf den Lebensstil dieses gastfreundlichen Volkes. Wir überließen uns dem Insel-Hopping, liefen an den weißesten Stränden der Welt entlang und tanzten zu lateinamerikanischer Musik. Die extrovertierte, auf Spaß ausgerichtete Art der Philippinen hat etwas Südamerikanisches. Wir reisten weiter nach Singapur, wo Kathy mich mit Designerfreunden bekannt machte, die mir die erstaunliche Eleganz des überaus wohlhabenden asiatischen Modellstaates vorführten. Die von ihnen gestalteten Häuser reflektieren durch die klaren minimalistischen Linien und Räume das Bedürfnis nach Ruhe und schaffen Inseln des Friedens in einer geschäftigen modernen Großstadt.

In Asien kann aus einem kurzen Flug rasch eine Zeitreise in die Vergangenheit werden. Myanmar ist ein armes rückständiges Land, das der Entwicklung in den Nachbarländern hinterher hinkt. Aber in den Klöstern und Pagoden sind Besucher sogar zu ihren heiligsten Zeremonien und Gebeten zugelassen. Tatsächlich bin ich nirgendwo in Asien an der Tür eines buddhistischen Denkmals abgewiesen worden. Myanmar ist noch unberührt und ursprünglich und die Menschen zugewandt, schüchtern und neugierig zugleich. Auf eine bezaubernde Weise offenbaren sie ihre Freude darüber, dass Besucher von so weit anreisen, um ihr Land zu besuchen. Wie so oft in Asien erfahren wir Fremde hier viel Respekt und Aufmerksamkeit, und die Einwohner von Myanmar strahlen eine erfrischende Unschuld aus, wie ich sie selten erlebt habe.

Bis Februar 2004 hatte sich so viel unterschiedliches Fotomaterial angehäuft, dass aus dem ursprünglich geplanten einbändigen Buch »Eastern Interiors« nun »Inside Asia« in zwei Bänden werden sollte. Die neue Planung bedeutete eine wesentlich größere Herausforderung, die über private Einrichtungsstile weit hinausging. Das neue Projekt sollte auch die »Sangha« der buddhistischen Mönche und Nonnen sowie die bedeutendsten buddhistischen Stätten umfassen. Natürlich saß ich begeistert in den Startlöchern, musste jedoch auch die doppelte Arbeit erledigen – bei unverändertem Abgabetermin. Aber schließlich linderten asiatische Massage und Akupunktur meine Nackenschmerzen. Verbunden mit intensivem Schwimmen, Yoga und Konzentration auf die Aufgabe war dies die beste Therapie. Statt mich am grünen Tisch endlos vorzubereiten, vertraute ich meiner Intuition und folgte meinem Instinkt. Am nächsten Tag saß ich wieder im Flieger: insgesamt 67 mal in sieben Monaten. Ich stellte fest, dass ich nur mit dem Strom schwimmen und mich auf meine grenzenlose Neugier und die angemessene Portion Glück verlassen musste. So gelangte ich an Orte, die ich mir nie hätte vorstellen können.

Der Flug von Luang Prabang wurde mehrmals verschoben, weil überall in Laos die Reisfelder in Flammen standen. Stadt und Land leuchteten surreal in gelbem Rauch. Mit dem Segen von Grand Satou, dem Oberhaupt der laotischen Buddhisten, durfte ich am strengen, würdevollen Leben der Mönche und Novizen in den Klöstern von Laos teilnehmen. Architekten, die für die Unesco arbeiteten, zeigten mir den komplexen Entwurf der offiziellen Königsresidenz, eines architektonischen Juwels an der Mündung des Mekons. In der Luft liegt der Geist des alten Indochina, als sei die Zeit stehen geblieben.

In Kambodscha zog ich Kathy in der Tempelanlage von Angkor Wat mit in ungeahnte Höhen. Sie hatte schreckliche Höhenangst, aber ich bestand darauf, dass sie ihre Furcht überwand. Schließlich hatte sie die einmalige Gelegenheit, das geheimnisvollste und großartigste Denkmal zu erklimmen, das je von Menschenhand erbaut wurde. Den Gipfel zu erreichen und die ausgedehnte heilige Stadt, die ganz und gar dem spirituellen Leben geweiht war, von oben zu betrachten, war ein so einmaliges Erlebnis, das alle Anstrengungen wert war. Die in großem Stil erbauten Ruinen liegen mitten in einem Dschungel, Bäume und Wurzeln überwuchern die hinduistischen und buddhistischen Tempel und Statuen. Die vollkommenen Kunstwerke in Stein verkörpern das Göttliche, das über die Zeit erhaben ist. Warum solch eine großartige Stadt, eine Zivilisation mit derart hoch entwickelter Fähigkeit zu Kultur und Weisheit einfach verschwinden und sechshundert Jahre lang vergessen werden konnte, bleibt rätselhaft. Wir erkundeten das große Tempelgelände in einem Jeep aus jener Epoche, die hier als »American War« bezeichnet wird. Das Land, das zunächst von den Vietcong überrannt, dann von den Roten Khmer zurückerobert und schließlich von kambodschanischen Truppen eingenommen wurde, war in der jüngeren Geschichte Opfer unvorstellbarer Grausamkeiten. Das Trauma ist allgegenwärtig, so lange noch Kinder herzzerreißende Geschichten erzählen. Dennoch blickt das Volk hoffnungsvoll und mutig in die Zukunft, denn die Kambodschaner besinnen sich auf ihre traditionellen Fähigkeiten, erwecken die Kunst zu neuem Leben und setzen auf den Tourismus, um ihr Land aus dem Elend zu befreien.

Der älteste Tempel Hanois erhob sich wie eine kleine Insel aus dem Dunst eines Sees. Novizen in dunkelbraunen Kutten öffneten die Tore zu den großen Innenhöfen. Das Haus von Mr. Ahn ließ eine Prinzessin, deren Bild im Schrein der Familie verehrt wird, nach den Prinzipien des Feng Shui erbauen. Danach beruht eine ausgeglichene Harmonie weitgehend auf dem Umgang mit den Elementen, vor allem mit Wind und Wasser. Die guten Energien müssen fließen, während die schlechten abgewehrt werden. Der Cousin des letzten Kaisers Baudai holte in seinem schlichten Haus innerhalb der Zitadelle die ehemaligen Hofgewänder aus einer Kiste unter dem Bett hervor. Der alte Mann führte mich auch durch die »Verbotene Purpurne Stadt«, in der er seine Kindheit verbracht hatte. Im Inneren der wenigen Gebäude, die nicht den amerikanischen Bomben zum Opfer gefallen sind, begrüßten ihn jene, die ihn erkannten, mit tiefen Verbeugungen, während andere sich über den alten Mann in schäbigen Seidengewändern lustig machten. Während er sich mit Tränen in den Augen an das Leben bei Hofe und geheime Türen und Gänge erinnerte, dachte ich, dass das Leben des »Letzten Kaisers« von China nicht viel anders verlaufen sein konnte.

Inzwischen machte Sunil in Japan bei seinen langen Vorbereitungen vollkommen andere Erfahrungen. In einem Land, in dem es nicht üblich ist, andere zu sich nach Hause einzuladen, erschien es unerhört, einen fotografierenden »gaijin« (japanisch für Ausländer) zu empfangen. Zum Höhepunkt des japanischen Wirtschaftswunders um 1980 lebte ich 18 Monate in Tokio und bin daher mit den vielschichtigen Ausprägungen der japanischen Gesellschaft vertraut. Aufgrund langer historisch bedingter Abgrenzungstendenzen hat sich Japan zu einer sehr eigenen Zivilisation entwickelt, und es überraschte mich nicht, dass sich in der langen Zeit meiner Abwesenheit an den Einstellungen und Lebensstilen kaum etwas geändert hatte. Die meisten Menschen in diesem reichsten und fortgeschrittensten Land Asiens leben in winzigen Wohnungen in endlosen neonbeleuchteten Vorstädten. Auf der Bahnfahrt im »Shinkansen« von Tokio nach Osaka erlebt man mit eigenen Augen den traurigen Tribut, den die Gesellschaft für die völlig verfehlte Städteplanung, die rücksichtslose Zerstörung der traditionellen Infrastruktur und das Zurückdrängen der Natur bezahlen muss. Die Besessenheit einer einzigen Generation für Fortschritt und Wirtschaftswachstum führte zu einer weitgehenden Zerstörung der japanischen Landschaft. Heutzutage erkennen die Japaner, welchen hohen Preis sie bezahlen mussten. Der amerikanische Schriftsteller Alex Kerr bemüht sich intensiv um die Erhaltung des japanischen Erbes. Seine beiden traditionellen Häuser, eins auf dem Gelände eines Shintoschreins nahe Kyotos, das andere ein altes Bauernhaus in dem abgelegenen Iya-Tal, stehen beispielhaft für die Wiederbelebung einer Ästhetik, die früher zum japanischen Alltag gehörte. Glücklicherweise ist diese Ästhetik auch in die radikale Architektur solch genialer Architekten wie Tadao Ando oder Kengo Kuma eingeflossen, die Zen-Prinzipien auch auf so grobes Baumaterial wie Beton anwenden.

China überraschte mich mit mitreißender Dynamik. Das Land, das mir zwanzig Jahre zuvor arm und düster vorgekommen war, hatte sich enorm verändert. Die Entwicklung zur Supermacht in punkto Produktivität hatte großen Einfluss auf das Leben vieler Chinesen. »Bereichert Euch«, lehrte einst Konfuzius, ein Grundsatz, den die kommunistische Partei der Volksrepublik geradezu verinnerlicht hatte. Vierhundert Millionen Chinesen ließen nun ihre Armut hinter sich. Weltwirtschaftsexperten beten für politische Stabilität in China, während sich jeder im neuesten Eldorado ein Stück vom Kuchen sichern will. Als ich den schicken China Club in Peking besuchte, traf ich dort auch Giorgio Armani, Dick Cheney und Condoleezza Rice an. In Begleitung von Renée Zellweger feierte Anthony Minghella im Club die Premiere seines Films »Unterwegs nach Cold Mountain«. In Shanghai wurden im letzten Jahrzehnt zweitausend Hochhäuser gebaut, und der »Bund« in der früheren englischen Konzession entwickelte sich zu einem von westlichem Luxus geprägten Boulevard der Eleganz. Entlang der Großen Mauer riefen Architekten die »Gemeinde an der Großen Mauer« ins Leben, ein ehrgeiziges Projekt, das China seinen Platz unter den großen Architektur- und Design-Nationen sichern soll. Global findet das Label »Made in China« immer mehr Anerkennung. Die Privathäuser der aus Europa stammenden Ausländer erscheinen dagegen wie eine nostalgische Hommage an die untergegangene Kultur des kaiserlich geprägten China.

Karma, mein Führer im Himalaja, zeigte mir die bedeutendsten Heiligtümer an Tibets heiligen Stätten. Die dunkle, verrauchte Atmosphäre im Innersten des tibetischen Buddhismus wirkt außerordentlich beeindruckend und bewegend. Alte und junge Pilger, Dorfbewohner und Nomaden strömen auf den Ladeflächen der Lastwagen, zu Fuß oder sich wiederholt niederwerfend über hunderte von Kilometern nach Lhasa. Die verwitterten, freundlichen Gesichter sind geprägt von dem harten Leben im hochgelegenen Himalaja, wo alles von einem geheimnisvollen Nebel umsponnen ist. Beim Anblick der tief verehrten, von Göttern und Dämonen bewachten Buddhas leuchten ihre Augen auf und spiegeln den innigen Glauben wider. Karma erzählte mir zahlreiche Geheimnisse und Legenden über Tibet, wo der Buddhismus seit über tausend Jahren jeden Aspekt des Lebens durchdringt. Hier wird schon den geringsten Ereignissen wie veränderten Windverhältnissen oder seltsamen Wolkenbildungen metaphysische Bedeutung zugesprochen. Im tantrischen Buddhismus hängen esoterische Rituale und Meditation eng zusammen, zumal Rituale und Musik in den renovierten Tempeln vorgeführt werden und die Klöster sich zunehmend mit lernbegierigen Schülern füllen. Im Jokhang-Tempel ließ Karma mich zuschauen, als er Jobo, der heiligsten Buddhafigur Tibets, Opfer darbrachte und betete. Während ich mit anderen Pilgern Schlange stand, um den Segen zu empfangen, wünschte ich mir einen Regenbogen. Als ich später die Sommerresidenz des Dalai Lama besichtigte, verdunkelte sich plötzlich der Himmel, und ein Gewitter entlud sich. Ich flüchtete ins Hotel, stieg aufs Dach und entdeckte den schönen Regenbogen über der Altstadt. Karma sah darin ein gutes Omen, und da Licht in der Fotografie eine Schlüsselrolle spielt, erkannte auch ich den darin verborgenen Symbolgehalt.

Ich flog wieder nach Indien und fuhr erneut Auto, möglicherweise in der Absicht, eventuell verbliebene Dämonen zu konfrontieren, die seit meinem Unfall in mir hätten schlummern können. Ich konnte aber nichts finden, alles war verschwunden: der Schmerz, die Schuldzuweisung, die Reue, die Alpträume. Ich hatte mein Schicksal akzeptiert, meine Lektion gelernt und mich dahingehend weiterbewegt, dass ich eins der besten Jahre meines Leben erleben durfte. Darin fand ich ein Gefühl der Befreiung, ja des Friedens.

Eine positive Einstellung ist wichtig – dem würden die meisten Asiaten zustimmen –, mir hat sie viele zauberhafte Augenblicke mit alten und neuen Freunden eingebracht, mit herzerwärmenden Erfahrungen an erstaunlichen Orten. »Inside Asia« hatte überdies einen positiven Einfluss auf alle, die an dem Buch mitgearbeitet haben. Agi Simões, der seit acht Jahren mit mir zusammenarbeitet, hat mir auch bei diesem Projekt wieder sehr geholfen. Jetzt hat er so viel Zutrauen zu sich selbst, dass er seine eigene Fotografenkarriere vorantreiben will. Für Angelika wurde die Herausgabe dieses Buches zu einem Akt der Meditation, währenddessen sie sich sämtlichen äußeren Einflüssen entzog, wie sie mir später erzählte. Wir alle waren seltsam berührt von dem guten Karma, das diesem Buch offensichtlich gegeben ist.

»Inside Asia« ist kein Buch über den Buddhismus. Der Buddhismus ist nicht an Orte gebunden, sondern wohnt in den Herzen der Menschen. Dies ist eher eine Reise an wunderschöne Orte von großer Harmonie, wo Weisheit und Philosophie des Buddhismus das Wohnen und Leben der Menschen durchdringen.

Um die Intensität und die Authentizität des jeweiligen Ambiente der über ganz Asien verteilten Wohnbereiche widerzuspiegeln, habe ich »Inside Asia« nur bei Tageslicht bzw. dem jeweils vorhandenen Licht mit konventionellem Filmmaterial fotografiert. Inhalt und Stimmung der Fotos bleiben unangetastet, da weder retuschiert noch digital korrigiert wurde.

Au fil de l'eau : voyage au cœur de l'Asie

Reto Guntli

L'Asie a joué un rôle important dans ma vie d'adulte. Une vraie passion pour ce continent exotique et ses habitants ainsi qu'un vif intérêt pour la philosophie et le mysticisme orientaux m'ont amené à passer quelques années en Asie quand j'avais une petite vingtaine d'années. J'y suis souvent retourné par la suite. Aussi, quand Angelika Taschen m'a proposé de participer aux « Eastern Interiors », alors que je travaillais au livre « The Hotel Book. Great Escapes », l'idée m'a enthousiasmé d'emblée.

En avril 2003, je me suis rendu à Delhi pour discuter avec Sunil Sethi, l'auteur de cet ouvrage, de notre future collaboration. Mais une visite au Taj Mahal a tourné au cauchemar, changeant le cours des événements. Grièvement blessé dans un accident de voiture, j'ai eu la vie sauve grâce à un sauvetage dans les plus grandes douleurs et à mon rapatriement en avion en Suisse, où j'ai subi une opération des cervicales. Pendant mes longs mois de convalescence à la maison, j'ai eu tout loisir de réfléchir et je suis parvenu à la conclusion qu'il fallait prendre la vie comme elle venait et en tirer le meilleur parti possible. En me concentrant sur les améliorations qu'apportait chaque jour, j'ai donné à l'avenir un tout autre sens. J'avais une seconde chance dans la vie et j'en étais reconnaissant. Il m'avait fallu cette expérience douloureuse pour réfléchir à ces vérités. Comme je me disais que je devais être reconnaissant pour chaque jour que je vivais, une vitalité nouvelle semblait m'animer. Accepter l'idée que rien au monde ne doit être considéré comme une évidence allait me donner la clé d'expériences et de joies inattendues.

Trois mois plus tard – après avoir retiré ma minerve – j'ai pris l'avion pour Bali. Cette île exotique était devenue ma retraite depuis que j'y avais séjourné à l'âge de 19 ans. Cette époque bouillonnante de liberté avait eu une influence durable sur ma vie ultérieure. Au plus profond de moi, j'ai toujours cherché à préserver cette légèreté partout où je suis allé. Tous les voyageurs qui, comme moi, ont découvert Bali à la fin des années 1970, voulaient y rester pour toujours. Nous étions séduits par la végétation tropicale luxuriante et le charme de ses habitants chaleureux et d'une grande douceur. Certains d'entre nous – comme Anita Lococo, dont l'amitié indéfectible a maintenu vivant le lien avec cette île – se sont installés à Bali. Aujourd'hui, Anita loue des maisons de vacances sous les tropiques à des voyageurs et des stars du rock. Bali est une vitrine de l'architecture et du design les plus novateurs d'Asie, et Anita et moi nous nous assurons que je prenne un bon départ. Aujourd'hui encore, il émane des rituels esthétiques et mystérieux de Bali une profonde spiritualité. La vie quotidienne, la religion et la nature ne font qu'un dans le cosmos des Balinais. Profonds, sincères et pleins d'humour, ils affrontent la vie avec une très grande aisance. On peut beaucoup apprendre de leurs manières simples et vraies.

Lorsque Angelika Taschen a visionné à Berlin mes premiers photoreportages de Bali, elle s'est rendu compte que les maisons des habitants, que ce soit en ville ou à la campagne, reflétaient les valeurs bouddhiques telles que l'harmonie et la sérénité. C'est ainsi que le bouddhisme est devenu le thème central de ce livre. Personnellement fortement attirée par les civilisations et le mysticisme asiatiques, Angelika a fait un remarquable travail d'éditrice au fur et à mesure que les photographies arrivaient à flots de toutes les régions d'Asie.

De la plantation de café à Java aux quartiers historiques de la Malaysia, en passant par des îles privées des Philippines ou même des résidences dans la banlieue de Manille ou de Singapour, des matériaux naturels, l'art bouddhique et les espaces méditatifs zen ont montré la nécessité d'aborder l'habitat d'une manière contemplative, authentique, voire spirituelle.

Mon amie Kathy de Guzman, charmante femme du monde et grande voyageuse, m'a emmené dans ses Philippines natales à la découverte des styles de vie des personnes les plus hospitalières qui soient. Nous avons fait des sauts de puce d'île en île, foulé les plages au sable le plus blanc du monde et dansé sur des musiques latino-américaines. Nous avons ensuite mis le cap sur Singapour, pour rencontrer le « vivier » d'architectes et de designers que Kathy compte parmi ses amis. Le pays modèle très prospère d'Asie nous a éblouis par sa sophistication. L'habitat contemporain, îlots de paix dans la ville moderne trépidante, y reflète la recherche de quiétude par le biais de lignes et espaces minimalistes. En Asie, un vol entre deux pays tient souvent du voyage avec la machine à remonter le temps.

Le Myanmar est un pays pauvre et arriéré, qui n'est pas développé comme ses voisins. Mais sa beauté est à vous couper le souffle et son patrimoine est extraordinaire. Les visiteurs sont bienvenus. Le Myanmar est encore préservé et authentique, et les Birmans sont affectueux, timides et curieux. Ils ont une manière charmante de montrer qu'ils sont ravis de voir des gens venir de si loin pour visiter leur pays. Comme c'est souvent le cas en Asie, ils traitent les étrangers avec grand respect et les entourent d'attentions. Les habitants du Myanmar ont une innocence rafraîchissante comme on n'en rencontre guère ailleurs.

En février 2004, on disposait de documents photographiques si nombreux et si variés que « Inside Asia », titre en deux tomes, est venu remplacer « Eastern Interiors » en un volume prévu à l'origine. Nous avions à relever un plus grand défi : outre les intérieurs privés et les styles, cet ouvrage devait aussi aborder la Sangha, à savoir la communauté des moines et des religieuses bouddhistes, ainsi que les monuments sacrés bouddhiques majeurs. Débordant d'énergie et impatient de partir, je me retrouvais devant le double de travail à effectuer dans les mêmes délais. Les massages asiatiques et l'acupuncture ont contribué d'abord à atténuer mes douleurs cervicales, puis à les éliminer. Conjugués à beaucoup de natation, de yoga et de concentration sur ma tâche, cela a été la meilleure thérapie. Plutôt que de consacrer beaucoup de temps à des préparations interminables, je me fiais à mes intuitions, suivais mon instinct et prenais spontanément l'avion : 67 vols au total en l'espace de sept mois. Me laisser porter par les flots s'est révélé être le bon choix ; une curiosité sans bornes et une chance immense feraient le reste. Cet état d'esprit m'a amené dans des endroits dont je ne soupçonnais pas même l'existence.

Les vols en partance de Luang Prabang ont été annulés à plusieurs reprises, en raison d'incendies embrasant les rizières dans tout le Laos. La fumée donnait à la ville et ses alentours un rougeoiement jaune irréel. Avec la bénédiction du très vénéré « Grand Satou », le chef de la communauté bouddhiste du Laos, j'ai pu partager la vie disciplinée et raffinée des moines et novices dans les temples et monastères, lieux de pèlerinage. Des architectes de l'Unesco m'ont montré la qualité architecturale de la cité royale officielle, une merveille construite dans un méandre du Mékong. C'est un endroit où le temps s'est arrêté et sur lequel plane la nostalgie de l'Indochine.

Au Cambodge, j'ai traîné Kathy au sommet du temple en ruine d'Angkor Vat à des hauteurs prodigieuses. Elle souffrait de vertige, mais je n'ai pas lâché prise : elle devait braver et surmonter sa peur, car elle avait la possibilité d'escalader le monument le plus mystérieux et le plus impressionnant jamais fait par l'homme. Parvenir au sommet et découvrir la cité sacrée s'étalant à ses pieds a vraiment procuré à Kathy une émotion récompensant largement son effort. Ce gigantesque ensemble de temples hindouistes ou bouddhistes et de sculptures géantes en ruine est enfoui dans une jungle de branchages et racines à la croissance exubérante. Ces œuvres d'art parfaites, principe divin fait pierre, défient le temps. Comment un endroit d'une telle magnificence et une civilisation si raffinée et d'une telle sagesse ont pu tout simplement disparaître et être oubliés pendant six cents ans demeure un mystère. Nous avons exploré l'immense enceinte du temple dans une jeep américaine de l'époque que l'on appelle ici la « Guerre américaine ». Pris par le Viêt-cong, repris par les Khmers rouges, puis par les troupes cambodgiennes, ce pays a vécu une histoire récente cruelle à laquelle renvoyait notre véhicule. Le Cambodge n'a pas encore pansé ses plaies : des enfants vous racontent des histoires à vous fendre le cœur. Mais ce peuple est animé d'un grand espoir et d'une forte volonté d'aller de l'avant. Les Cambodgiens réapprennent leurs métiers et font revivre leurs arts, dans l'espoir que le tourisme favorisera le développement de leur pays. La jeep appartient maintenant au Amansara Resort.

Le plus vieux temple d'Hanoi est un îlot s'élevant au-dessus de la brume. Des novices en habit brun foncé nous en ont ouvert les portes sur de vastes cours. A Hué la maison de M. Ahna été construite selon les principes du Feng Shui par une princesse, dont le portrait est exposé sur l'autel familial. Selon cet art traditionnel, l'harmonie serait étroitement liée aux éléments naturels, le vent et l'eau en particulier. Les énergies positives doivent circuler, tandis que les énergies négatives doivent être arrêtées, – l'atmosphere paisable tient aux flots de «chi», l'énergie qui se trouve en toutes choses. D'ailleurs, les seuls papillons que j'ai vus au Viêt-nam voletaient tous dans le jardin de M. Ahn. Son ami, fonctionnaire et poète, écrit ses poèmes, retiré dans la «Peaceful Mansion», sur les rives de la Rivière aux parfums. Les guerres n'ont pas entamé la passion des Vietnamiens pour la littérature : même de grands temples sont dédiés à cet art. Dans sa modeste demeure dans l'enceinte de la citadelle, un cousin du dernier empereur Bao Dai a sorti ses habits de cour d'un coffre rangé sous son lit. Le vieil homme m'a fait visiter la «Cité pourpre interdite», dans laquelle il avait passé toute son enfance. Dans les quelques édifices ayant survécu aux bombardements américains, les personnes qui le connaissaient esquissaient une révérence, tandis que les autres considéraient d'un œil amusé cet homme vêtu d'atours en guenilles. Alors qu'il racontait la vie à la Cour, les yeux brillants en évoquant les portes dérobées et les passages secrets, il m'est soudain apparu que le destin du «dernier empereur de Chine » n'avait pas dû être très différent.

Pendant ce temps, Sunil vivait toute autre chose au Japon, où il a consacré de nombreuses semaines à ses travaux préparatoires. Dans ce pays où il n'est pas de mise de recevoir chez soi, accueillir un photographe «gaijin», comme les Japonais appellent les étrangers, était chose inouïe. Au faîte du miracle économique japonais dans les années 1980, j'avais passé 18 mois à Tokyo et les subtilités de la société japonaise ne me sont pas étrangères. Une histoire marquée par l'isolationnisme a fait du Japon une civilisation à part et je n'ai pas été surpris de ne trouver pratiquement aucun changement dans les comportements et le mode de vie après toutes ces années d'absence. La majorité des habitants du pays le plus prospère et le plus avancé d'Asie vivent dans de minuscules habitations cubiques en béton dans des banlieues tentaculaires éclairées par des enseignes au néon. Ce que l'on voit par la fenêtre du Shinkansen, le train qui assure la liaison entre Tokyo et Osaka, est un triste témoignage de l'absence alarmante d'urbanisme, de la destruction irréfléchie des infrastructures traditionnelles et du recul de la nature. L'obsession d'une génération pour le progrès et le développement économique a changé le paysage du tout au tout. Aujourd'hui, les Japonais commencent à se rendre compte du prix élevé qu'ils ont payé. Certaines personnes, dont l'écrivain américain Alex Kerr, ont cependant à cœur de préserver l'héritage japonais. Les maisons traditionnelles de Kerr, l'une dans un sanctuaire shintoïste près de Kyoto et l'autre, une vieille ferme, dans la vallée retirée d'Iya, sont de rares exemples du sens de l'esthétique dont était autrefois empreinte la vie quotidienne au Japon. Heureusement, cette esthétique se retrouve dans les créations radicales d'architectes de génie comme Tadao Ando ou Kengo Kuma qui insufflent l'esprit « zen » à des matériaux aussi bruts que le béton.

La Chine m'a surpris par sa vitalité et son dynamisme. Le pays que j'avais perçu comme morne et pauvre il y a une vingtaine d'années a donné naissance à une nouvelle Chine. Son accession fulgurante au statut de superpuissance de la productivité a eu un impact considérable sur la vie de nombreux Chinois. «Enrichissez-vous», professait Confucius et le Parti communiste de la république populaire de Chine a repris le message à son compte et fort à propos. En l'espace d'une décennie seulement, quatre cents millions de Chinois ont tiré un trait sur la pauvreté. Les économistes appellent de leurs vœux une Chine stable, tandis que tout le monde veut avoir sa part du gâteau dans le dernier eldorado. De passage au très chic China Club de Pékin, j'ai rencontré Giorgio Armani, Dick Cheney et Condoleezza Rice. Anthony Minghella y a célébré la première de son film «Retour à Cold Mountain», accompagné de Renée Zellweger. deux mille gratte-ciel ont été construits à Shanghai en l'espace d'une décennie. Le «Bund», dans l'ancienne concession britannique, est devenu un boulevard empreint de luxe occidental et de sophistication. A proximité d'un tronçon de la Grande Muraille, des architectes ont créé la «Commune de la Grande Muraille», projet dont l'ambition est de faire accéder la Chine au gotha de l'architecture et du design. «Made in China» se voit maintenant dans le monde entier. Les maisons des expatriés européens, en revanche, rendent un hommage nostalgique à la Chine impériale disparue.

Karma, mon guide dans l'Himalaya, m'a emmené dans les sanctuaires intérieurs des lieux sacrés tibétains. Entrer dans l'intimité sombre et enfumée du bouddhisme tibétain est une expérience profondément mystérieuse et émouvante. Des flots de pèlerins, villageois et nomades de tout âge arrivent à l'arrière de camions ou à pied, se prosternant parfois sur des centaines de kilomètres vers Lhassa. Les difficiles conditions de vie en altitude dans l'Himalaya, où tout est marqué au sceau du mystère, de la tragédie et du sens, sont gravées en profondeur dans les visages burinés et amicaux. Leurs yeux brillent d'une dévotion des plus ardentes devant les bouddhas faisant l'objet d'une grande vénération, gardés par des divinités et des démons. Karma m'a raconté nombre de secrets et légendes du Tibet, où le bouddhisme fait partie intégrante de la vie depuis un millénaire. C'est un endroit où des phénomènes naturels tels que le moindre changement de direction du vent ou dans la forme d'un nuage ont une signification métaphysique. Dans le bouddhisme tantrique, des rituels ésotériques sont étroitement associés à la méditation. Des cérémonies religieuses accompagnées de musique ont lieu dans des temples fraîchement rénovés et les monastères accueillent un nombre croissant de disciples avides d'étudier. Karma m'a invité à être auprès de lui tandis qu'il priait et faisait ses offrandes à Jowo Sakyamuni, la représentation la plus sacrée du Bouddha du Tibet au sein du temple du Jokhang. Alors que j'étais dans les rangs des pèlerins pour recevoir la bénédiction, j'ai fait le vœu de voir un arc-en-ciel. Plus tard dans la journée, dans la résidence d'été du dalaï-lama, une soudaine tempête de sable a obscurci le ciel bleu et un orage a éclaté. J'ai trouvé refuge à l'hôtel et je suis monté sur le toit. C'est alors que j'ai vu un splendide arc-en-ciel au dessus de Lhassa. Karma a interprété cela comme un signe de grande chance. Si l'on pense que la lumière est l'élément clé de la photographie, cet épisode était chargé de symbolisme.

Je suis retourné en Inde et me suis installé au volant d'une voiture, sans doute avec l'intention de regarder en face des démons qui pouvaient encore m'obséder depuis mon accident. Mais je ne les pas trouvés, ils avaient disparus : fini les douleurs, les reproches, les regrets et les cauchemars. J'avais accepté mon destin, en avais tiré les enseignements et étais entré dans l'une des meilleures années de ma vie. J'y trouvais un sentiment de libération, voire la paix.

Cette attitude positive – et la majorité des Asiatiques seraient d'accord avec moi – me réservait de nombreuses heures magiques en compagnies d'amis, de plus ou moins longue date, et d'innombrables expériences dans les endroits les plus inattendus. «Inside Asia» a aussi eu une influence très positive sur les professionnels qui ont travaillé à ce livre. Agi Simões, qui travaille avec moi depuis huit ans m'a secondé efficacement et a acquis suffisamment de confiance en soi pour se lancer dans une carrière de photographe indépendant. Pour Angelika, l'édition de cet ouvrage qu'elle voulait être un feu d'artifice est devenu un acte méditatif par lequel elle se soustrayait à toute influence extérieure, comme elle me l'a plus tard confié. Tout le monde est mystérieusement touché par le karma positif manifeste de ce livre.

«Inside Asia» ne prétend pas être un livre sur le bouddhisme, car celui-ci n'est pas lié à des lieux, il se trouve dans le cœur des êtres humains. Il s'agit plutôt d'un voyage vers des endroits rayonnant de beauté et d'harmonie, où la sagesse et la philosophie bouddhistes ont pénétré l'habitat et la vie des gens.

Pour rendre compte de l'intensité et de l'authenticité des diverses atmosphères des intérieurs, j'ai pris toutes les photos de «Inside Asia» à la lumière du jour, ou du moins en éclairage naturel, sur des pellicules classiques. Les sujets et les atmosphères des photos sont fidèles à la réalité, car je n'ai ni retouché ni corrigé numériquement.

TIBET

Jokhang Temple
Sakya Monastery

Potala Palace

Lhasa

The splendour of the Dalai Lama's seat.

Soaring above the eminence of Red Hill in the Tibetan capital, the thousand-roomed Potala Palace with its labyrinth of corridors and courtyards is the official seat of the Dalai Lama, Holder of the White Lotus.

Tibetans believe the Dalai Lama to be the earthly embodiment of the Bodhisattva of Compassion; for them the Potala is both a symbol of spiritual power and political freedom. Until his exile to India in 1959, the present Dalai Lama, fourteenth in line of reincarnates of the Gelugpa order of Buddhism, lived here. The palace was largely a reconstruction undertaken by the fifth Dalai Lama from 1645 onwards on the site of an earlier palace built by Songsten Gampo, the king who unified Tibet and ushered in Buddhism early in the seventh century. The Potala was a humming universe of throne rooms, offices, chapels and tombs of earlier Dalai Lamas. After the building of Norbulingka, the summer palace, in the 18th century, it was only used in winter months. But with the God-King gone, both palaces now echo with the drone of tourists.

Hoch über der Anhöhe des Roten Hügels in der tibetischen Hauptstadt ragt der Potala-Palast mit seinen tausend Zimmern und dem Labyrinth aus Gängen und Höfen empor – die offizielle Residenz des Dalai Lama, dem Herrn des Weißen Lotus.

Die Tibeter sehen im Dalai Lama die irdische Verkörperung des Bodhisattva des Mitleids, während der Potala-Palast als Symbol spiritueller Kraft und politischer Freiheit verehrt wird. Bis zum Gang ins indische Exil 1959 lebte hier auch die vierzehnte Inkarnation des buddhistischen Gelugpa-Ordens, der heutige Dalai Lama. Der Palast stellt größtenteils eine Rekonstruktion dar, die der fünfte Dalai Lama ab 1645 an der Stelle eines älteren Palastes vorantrieb. Dieser war von Songsten Gampo erbaut worden, dem König, der bereits im frühen 7. Jahrhundert Tibet befreit und den Buddhismus eingeführt hatte. Der Potala-Palast beherbergte ein geschäftiges Universum – mit Inthronisierungshallen, Amtsstuben und Kapellen sowie Grabstätten ehemaliger Dalai Lamas. Nachdem im 18. Jahrhundert die Sommerresidenz in Norbulingka gebaut wurde, nutzte der Dalai Lama den Potala nur noch im Winter. Da er heute gar nicht mehr in Tibet lebt, sind es die Touristen, die beide Paläste mit Leben füllen.

S'élevant au sommet de la Colline rouge, au cœur de la capitale tibétaine, le palais du Potala, dédale de couloirs, cours et pièces, est la résidence officielle du dalaï-lama, le seigneur du Lotus blanc.

Pour les Tibétains, le dalaï-lama est l'émanation terrestre du Bodhisattva de la compassion. Aussi voient-ils dans le Potala un symbole de pouvoir spirituel et de liberté politique. L'actuel dalaï-lama, le quatorzième supérieur de l'ordre des Gelugpas, y a vécu jusqu'à son exil en Inde en 1959. Le palais est en grande partie une reconstruction commencée en 1645 par le cinquième dalaï-lama sur le site d'un palais ancien, construit par Songtsen Gampo, l'artisan de l'unité tibétaine et l'initiateur du bouddhisme au Tibet au début du 7e siècle. Le Potala, ensemble architectural composé de salles du trône, bureaux, chapelles et sépultures de dalaï-lamas, grouillait de monde jusqu'à la construction, au 18e siècle, du Norbulinka, le palais d'été. Il n'a plus alors été habité que pendant les mois d'hiver. Mais depuis le départ du dieu-roi, les deux palais sont emplis de la rumeur des touristes.

⁎ **PREVIOUS PAGES** The massive inward sloping white and ochre walls of the Potala Palace rise to 13 storeys and a height of a thousand feet above the valley floor. **BELOW** The courtyard of the White Palace inside the Potala leads to the private quarters of the 13th and 14th Dalai Lamas. **FACING PAGE** A worshipper burns fragrant herbs as a votive offering at a stupa, or *chorten*, at the rear entrance to the palace. ⁎ **VORHERGEHENDE DOPPELSEITE** Die mächtigen einwärts geneigten weißen und ockerfarbenen Mauern des Potala erheben sich in 13 Stockwerken 110 Meter hoch über das Tal. **UNTEN** Der Hof des Weißen Palastes innerhalb des Potala führt zu den Privatgemächern des 13. und 14. Dalai Lama. **RECHTE SEITE** Ein Gläubiger verbrennt Duftkräuter als Weiheopfer vor einem Stupa oder *Chörten* am Hintereingang des Palastes. ⁎ **DOUBLE PAGE PRECEDENTE** Culminant à plus de 300 mètres au-dessus de la vallée, le Potala à la façade blanche et ocre écrase le visiteur du haut de ses 13 étages. **CI-DESSOUS** C'est par la cour du Palais blanc que l'on accède aux appartements privés des 13e et 14e dalaï-lamas. **PAGE DE DROITE** Près de l'entrée arrière du palais, un fidèle brûle des herbes aromatiques en offrande au pied d'un stupa, appelé *chörten* au Tibet.

* **FACING PAGE** Entrance doorways to the private quarters of the Dalai Lamas are lined with a traditional Tibetan awning. **ABOVE** The courtyard is hung with black and white banners with the eternal knot, signifying the unity of things. **BELOW** A gilt-plated bronze snow lion guards the entrance to the private chambers of the Dalai Lamas. * **LINKE SEITE** Die Eingänge zu den Privatgemächern der Dalai Lamas sind mit traditionellen tibetischen Vorhängen verhängt. **OBEN** Der Innenhof ist mit schwarzweißen Bannern geschmückt, die das Symbol des unendlichen Knotens tragen und so an die Einheit der Dinge erinnern. **UNTEN** Ein vergoldeter Schneelöwe bewacht den Eingang zu den Privatgemächern des Dalai Lama. * **PAGE DE GAUCHE** Les entrées des appartements privés des dalaï-lamas sont tendues de marquises traditionnelles tibétaines. **CI-DESSUS** Les drapeaux noirs et blancs accrochés dans la cour en contrebas arborent le nœud éternel, symbole de l'unité des choses. **CI-DESSOUS** Un lion des neiges en bronze plaqué or monte la garde à l'entrée des appartements des dalaï-lamas.

※ **PREVIOUS PAGES** A colonnade in the Potala's main courtyard is painted with a pattern of stylised clouds. A plait of prayer flags hangs from a bronze knocker on a palace gate. **ABOVE** A young monk decorates the terrace outside his room with a popular print of the Potala Palace. **FACING PAGE** an elaborately decorated doorway to the private rooms of the 13th and 14th Dalai Lamas. ※ **VORHERGEHENDE DOPPELSEITE** Ein Säulengang im Haupthof des Potala ist mit einem Muster aus stilisierten Wolken bemalt. Am Palasttor hängt ein Zopf aus geflochtenen Gebetsfahnen an einem Türklopfer aus Bronze. **OBEN** Ein junger Mönch verziert die Terrasse vor seinem Zimmer mit einem beliebten Poster vom Potala. **RECHTE SEITE** Das prächtig geschmückte Tor zu den Privatgemächern des 13. und 14. Dalai Lama. ※ **DOUBLE PAGE PRECEDENTE** Les motifs peints sur la colonnade dans la cour principale du Potala sont des nuages stylisés. Des drapeaux de prière tressés agrémentent un heurtoir de bronze visible sur une porte du palais. **CI-DESSUS** Un jeune moine décore la terrasse de sa chambre avec une représentation du Potala très prisée au Tibet. **PAGE DE DROITE** Cette porte très richement ornée mène aux appartements privés des 13e et 14e dalaï-lamas.

施工重地 游人勿入

⁂ **FACING PAGE AND ABOVE** entrance and front view of Norbulingka, the summer palace, built by the seventh Dalai Lama in 1755. *Norbulingka* means "Jewel Park" and lies two miles west of the Potala Palace. One of Lhasa's great pageants was the annual move of the Dalai Lama from the Potala to Norbulingka each spring. It was from here that the present Dalai Lama fled to India disguised as a soldier in March 1959. **BELOW** entrance to the Sera monastery, established in 1419, on the northern edge of Lhasa. **FOLLOWING PAGES** Novice monks in Sera monastery's famous Debating Garden prepare for monastic examinations by staging mock debates. ⁂ **LINKE SEITE UND OBEN** Eingang und Fassade des Norbulingka, der Sommerresidenz, die 1755 unter dem 7. Dalai Lama erbaut wurde. *Norbulingka* bedeutet Juwelengarten und liegt etwa drei Kilometer westlich des Potala. Der jährliche Umzug des Dalai Lama vom Potala zum Norbulingka wurde in jedem Frühling feierlich begangen. Von hier aus floh der heutige Dalai Lama im März 1959 als Soldat verkleidet nach Indien. **UNTEN** Der Eingang zum Kloster Sera, das 1419 am nördlichen Rand von Lhasa gegründet wurde. **FOLGENDE DOPPELSEITE** Die Novizen bereiten sich im berühmten Disputationshof des Klosters Sera auf die Ordensprüfungen vor, indem sie die Debatten miteinander proben. ⁂ **PAGE DE GAUCHE ET CI-DESSUS** entrée et façade du Norbulinka, le palais d'été, construit par le 7e dalaï-lama en 1755. Le *Norbulinka*, dit « Parc du joyau précieux », est situé à trois kilomètres à l'ouest du Potala. Tous les ans, au printemps, le déménagement du dalaï-lama pour le Norbulinka était un spectacle fastueux. C'est de ce palais que, déguisé en soldat, le dalaï-lama s'est enfui en Inde en mars 1959. **CI-DESSOUS** l'entrée du monastère de Sera, fondé en 1419, à la lisière septentrionale de Lhassa. **DOUBLE PAGE SUIVANTE** Dans le célèbre jardin du monastère de Sera, des novices se préparent à des examens théologiques en simulant des débats dialectiques.

Jokhang Temple
Lhasa

Tibet's centre of sacred history and devotion.

Teeming with thousands of worshippers all day long, the continuous press of pilgrims prostrating, lighting butter lamps in chapels, making circumambulatory trips or taking in the view from its gilded rooftops, the Jokhang is the sacred centre of Tibet, its holiest of holies.

The temple's origins date back to the capital which King Songsten Gampo established at Lhasa in the seventh century. His two wives, a Chinese and a Nepali princess, are said to have brought images of the Buddha that converted the warrior king and introduced Buddhism to Tibet. The Jokhang is believed to be built on geomantic power points that pin down a sprawling ogress. Its innermost shrine contains the statue of Sakyamuni, the Historical Buddha, that came with the Chinese princess. Over the centuries the Jokhang has seen many changes, including much damage done during the Cultural Revolution. That has neither dimmed the fervour of devotees thronging from remote corners of Tibet, nor diluted the palimpsest of intense spirituality that pervades its smoky, mysterious, lamp-lit interiors.

Im Jokhang, dem heiligen Herz und Nationalheiligtum der tibetischen Kultur, trifft der nie versiegende Strom der Pilger auf tausende von Gläubigen. Die Besucher werfen sich demütig nieder, zünden Butterlampen an, wandeln auf Rundwegen oder bewundern die Aussicht von den vergoldeten Dächern.

Der Tempel geht auf die Zeit zurück, als König Songsten Gampo Lhasa im 7. Jahrhundert zur Hauptstadt ausbaute. Der Legende nach haben seine beiden Frauen, eine chinesische und eine nepalesische Prinzessin, Buddhafiguren nach Tibet mitgebracht, die den kriegerischen König zur inneren Umkehr und Einführung des Buddhismus veranlassten. Der Jokhang soll auf geomantischen Kraftfeldern über einer auf dem Rücken liegenden Riesin erbaut worden sein. Im Hauptsanktuarium befindet sich das Standbild des Sakyamuni, des historischen Buddha, das die chinesische Prinzessin mitbrachte. Im Laufe der Jahrhunderte war der Jokhang vielen Veränderungen unterworfen und wurde während der Kulturrevolution schwer beschädigt. Dem Eifer der Gläubigen selbst aus den entlegendsten Gegenden Tibets tat dies jedoch keinen Abbruch, und auch die tiefe Spiritualität der verräucherten, geheimnisvollen Innenräume blieb erhalten.

Du matin au soir, le Jokhang accueille des milliers de fidèles et une foule de pèlerins qui se prosternent, allument des lampes à beurre dans des chapelles, font des circumambulations ou admirent les toits dorés du château. Le Jokhang est le centre sacré du Tibet, son saint des saints.

Le temple remonte au 7e siècle, à l'époque où le roi Songsten Gampo a fait de Lhassa sa capitale. Ses deux épouses, une princesse chinoise et une princesse népalaise, auraient apporté avec elles des représentations du Bouddha. Celles-ci ont amené le roi-guerrier à se convertir et à introduire le bouddhisme au Tibet. Selon une croyance, le Jokhang aurait été bâti sur des points de géomancie clouant au sol une démone. Son sanctuaire intérieur recèle une statue de Sakyamuni, le Bouddha historique, apportée par la princesse chinoise. Au fil des siècles, le Jokhang a connu de nombreux changements, voire des dégradations importantes pendant la Révolution culturelle. Cela n'a cependant jamais fait décliner la ferveur des fidèles qui arrivent en foule des profondeurs du Tibet, ni estompé la spiritualité intense dont sont empreints ses espaces intérieurs brumeux, mystérieux, éclairés à la lueur de lampes.

* **PREVIOUS PAGES** Pilgrims enter the Jokhang through the southern entrance of the Barkor, the middle of the three ritual circuits that surround the temple and the city of Lhasa. The inner passage, known as Nangkhor, goes round the heart of the Jokhang. Each circumambulation is made in a clock-wise direction. **ABOVE** The Jokhang's rooftops of hand-beaten copper are gilded with gold. **FACING PAGE** Intricately modelled and gilded finials, images of guardian deities and sacred symbols decorate three levels of Jokhang's roofs. * **VORHERGEHENDE DOPPELSEITE** Die Pilger betreten den Jokhang durch den südlichen Eingang am Barkhor-Platz, der die Mitte der drei rituellen Rundgänge um den Tempel und die Stadt Lhasa markiert. Der innere Gang, der Nangkhor, verläuft um das Heiligtum. Jeder Rundgang ist im Uhrzeigersinn zu begehen. **OBEN** Die Dächer des Jokhang sind aus handgehämmertem vergoldetem Kupfer. **RECHTE SEITE** Prachtvoll geformte Spitzen, Figuren von Schutzgottheiten und heilige Symbole zieren die Dächer des Jokhang auf drei Ebenen. * **DOUBLE PAGE PRECEDENTE** Des pèlerins entrent dans le Jokhang par la porte sud du Barkhor, le parcours intermédiaire des trois circuits rituels entourant le temple et la ville de Lhassa. Le circuit intérieur, appelé Nangkor, cerne les chapelles intérieures du Jokhang. Les circumambulations s'effectuent dans le sens des aiguilles d'une montre. **CI-DESSUS** Les toits du Jokhang sont en cuivre martelé à la main et doré. **PAGE DE DROITE** Des épis de faîtage dorés très travaillés, des représentations de divinités protectrices et des symboles sacrés ornent les toitures du Jokhang.

* **PREVIOUS PAGES** a gold idol of Maitreya, the Future Buddha, richly adorned with jewels and silks. Detail of an inner sanctum door with bronze handles cast in the shape of gilded dragons. **ABOVE** a row of Sakyamunis, Historical Buddhas, in the inner sanctum of the Jokhang. * **VORHERGEHENDE DOPPELSEITE** ein goldenes, prunkvoll mit Edelsteinen und Seide geschmücktes Abbild des in Zukunft erscheinenden Buddha Maitreya. Detail einer Tür zum Hauptsanktuarium mit bronzenen Griffen in Form vergoldeter Drachen. **OBEN** mehrere Sakyamunis, historische Buddhas, im Hauptheiligtum des Jokhang. * **DOUBLE PAGE PRECEDENTE** Une statue dorée de Maitreya, le Bouddha des temps futurs, parée de bijoux et de soieries. La porte du sanctuaire intérieur est pourvue de poignées de bronze doré en forme de dragon. **CI-DESSUS** Le sanctuaire intérieur du Jokhang abrite une collection de Sakyamuni, bouddhas historiques.

※ **ABOVE** monks at prayer before a jewelled golden idol of Padmasambhava, also known as Guru Rinpoche, the 8th-century adept from the Indian subcontinent who helped to establish Buddhism in Tibet. He is regarded as the second Buddha by the Nyingmapa school of Buddhism. **FOLLOWING PAGES** Monks in the Jokhang's inner sanctum bundle currency notes left as offerings. Between the eaves and the colonnade is a row of sphinx-like snow lions, each carved with a human expression. These are thought to have been inspired by Persian images brought via Kashmir. ※ **OBEN** Mönche beten vor der prachtvoll mit Edelsteinen verzierten, goldenen Statue des Padmasambhava, der auch unter dem Namen Guru Rinpoche bekannt ist und im 8. Jahrhundert als Meister vom indischen Subkontinent dazu beitrug, den Buddhismus in Tibet zu begründen. Die Anhänger der buddhistischen Nyingmapa-Schule bezeichnen ihn als »Zweiten Buddha«. **FOLGENDE DOPPELSEITE** Die Mönche im Hauptsanktuarium des Jokhang bündeln die Geldscheine, die als Opfergaben gespendet wurden. Zwischen den Dachtraufen und dem Säulengang befinden sich sphinxartige Schneelöwenköpfe mit menschlich anmutendem Gesichtsausdruck. Als Vorbild gelten persische Statuen, die über Kaschmir nach Tibet gelangten. ※ **CI-DESSUS** des moines prient devant une statue dorée et parée de bijoux du Padmasambhava, aussi connu sous le nom de gourou Rinpoché. Ce fidèle originaire du sous-continent indien au 8e siècle a aidé le bouddhisme à prendre pied au Tibet. La tradition Nyingmapa le considère comme le deuxième bouddha. **DOUBLE PAGE SUIVANTE** Dans le sanctuaire intérieur du Jokhang, des moines mettent en liasse des billets de banque donnés en offrande. Entre les avant-toits et la colonnade, des lions des neiges aux airs de sphinx surprennent par leur expression humaine. Ils seraient inspirés de miniatures persanes arrivées au Tibet par le Cachemire.

※ **FACING PAGE** Pilgrims light oil lamps at a shrine facing the main entrance of the Jokhang on Barkhor Square. They burn fragrant herbs in clay ovens on certain auspicious days in votive offering. **ABOVE** the front of the Jokhang on Barkhor Square. **FOLLOWING PAGES** Women workers repair the roof of the Jokhang and, later, take an afternoon break. The complex of rooftop pavilions contains monks' quarters and workshops. Elaborately carved eaves with interlocking wooden joints are typical of classical Tibetan architecture. Detail of a snow lion between the wooden brackets and eaves. ※ **LINKE SEITE** Pilger entzünden Öllämpchen an einem Schrein am Haupteingang des Jokhang am Barkhor-Platz. An bestimmten verheißungsvollen Tagen verbrennen sie als Votivgaben Duftkräuter in Lehmöfen. **OBEN** die Fassade des Jokhang am Barkhor-Platz. **FOLGENDE DOPPELSEITEN** Frauen reparieren das Dach des Jokhang, am Nachmittag machen sie eine Pause. In diesem Komplex von Dachpavillons liegen die Wohnräume und Werkstätten der Mönche. Feingeschnitzte Dachtraufen mit zusammengesteckten Holzfugen sind charakteristisch für die tibetische Architektur. Detail eines Schneelöwen zwischen Konsolgebälk und Drachtraufen. ※ **PAGE DE GAUCHE** Des pèlerins allument des lampes à huile dans un sanctuaire situé face à l'entrée principale du Jokhang, sur la place du Barkhor. Certains jours favorables, les pèlerins brûlent, pour témoigner leur reconnaissance, des herbes aromatiques dans des fours en argile. **CI-DESSUS** la façade du Jokhang donnant sur la place du Barkhor. **DOUBLES PAGES SUIVANTES** Des ouvrières réparent le toit du Jokhang. On les voit plus tard dans l'après-midi, à l'heure de la pause. Ce complexe de pavillons aux toits pittoresques abrite les cellules des moines et les ateliers. Des avant-toits délicatement sculptés constitués de solives entrecroisées sont typiques de l'architecture tibétaine classique. un lion des neiges entre les consoles et les avant-toits.

Sakya Monastery Tsang

Western Tibet

A symbol of survival on the high road from Lhasa to Kathmandu.

"There was a sense in the little chapel of something timeless, that had kept Sakya going for centuries, regardless of the violent intermissions. I felt this was a remote, independent place, a place that was used to running its own affairs…," recorded the historian Patrick French when he visited Sakya monastery a few years ago.

Established in 1073 as the seat of the Sakyapa order of Buddhism, the monastery's head Sakya Pandita was the saintly eminence who won the patronage of Godan Khan, grandson of the invading Genghis Khan. Buddhism was declared the state religion of the Mongol empire and for about a hundred years, from the mid-13th century, the lamas of Sakya ruled Tibet. Unlike other Buddhist sects who choose their heads as incarnates, the abbots of Sakya are hereditary and come from one family. Large parts of the monastery were destroyed during the Cultural Revolution and the number of monks is now down to less than a hundred. But its grey walls, marked with distinctive red and white stripes, are a stirring symbol of survival against all odds.

»Die kleine Kapelle strahlte etwas Zeitloses aus, das Sakya jahrhundertelang ausgemacht hat, unabhängig von gewaltsamen Eindringlingen. Ich spürte, dass ich an einen abgelegenen, unabhängigen Ort gelangt war, einen Ort, der seinen eigenen Dingen nachging …«, berichtete der britische Historiker Patrick French, als er vor einigen Jahren das Kloster Sakya besuchte.

Sakya Pandita, der dem 1073 als Sitz der buddhistischen Sakyapa-Schule gegründeten Kloster vorstand, stand als heilige Eminenz unter dem Schutz von Dschingis Khans Enkel Göden. Der Buddhismus wurde zur Staatsreligion der Mongolei erklärt, und über hundert Jahre lang herrschten die Lamas von Sakya über Tibet. Im Gegensatz zu anderen buddhistischen Schulen, die ihre Oberhäupter als Inkarnationen wählen, vererben die Äbte von Sakya ihr Amt in der Familie weiter. Im Zuge der Kulturrevolution wurde das Kloster großenteils zerstört, und heute leben nur noch knapp hundert Mönche im Kloster. Doch die grauen Klostermauern, die markant rotweiß gestreift gestrichen wurden, bleiben das Symbol für das Überleben der Klosteranlage – allen Widrigkeiten zum Trotz.

«Il y avait, dans cette petite chapelle, quelque chose d'atemporel qui avait perpétué Sakya au fil des siècles, en dépit des intermèdes violents. Cet endroit m'a fait l'effet d'être lointain et coupé du reste du monde, de vivre en autarcie…», notait l'historien Patrick French lors de sa visite au monastère de Sakya, il y a quelques années.

Siège de l'ordre bouddhique des Sakyapas depuis sa création en 1073, ce monastère avait pour supérieur Sakya Pandita, le maître qui avait gagné à la cause du bouddhisme Godan Khan, petit-fils de l'envahisseur Gengis Kahn. Le bouddhisme a été proclamé religion officielle de l'empire mongol et, du milieu du 13e siècle au milieu du 14e siècle, les lamas de Sakya ont gouverné le Tibet. Contrairement à d'autres écoles bouddhistes qui recherchent les incarnations de leur chef, la charge de supérieur est héréditaire à Sakya. Des parties importantes du monastère ont été détruites pendant la Révolution culturelle et le nombre de moines vivant à Sakya est tombé à moins d'une centaine. Mais ses murs gris marqués de bandes rouges et blanches caractéristiques symbolisent la survivance du monastère malgré toutes les vicissitudes de l'histoire.

※ **FACING PAGE** the Kyichu River, swollen from melting snows, resembles a turquoise lake on the route from the Sakya monastery to Lhasa. **FACING PAGE** detail of rock relief at Nyethang. **ABOVE** A large image of the Sakyamuni, the Historical Buddha, is carved into a rock face in the small village of Nyethang on the road to Sakya. In front are clay ovens for the burning of herbs as votive offering. ※ **LINKE SEITE** Der breite, Tauwasser führende Fluss Kyichu ähnelt auf der Strecke vom Kloster Sakya nach Lhasa einem türkisfarbenen See. **LINKE SEITE** Detail des Felsreliefs in Nyethang. **OBEN** Eine große Statue des Sakyamuni, des historischen Buddha, wurde unweit des Dorfes Nyethang auf der Straße nach Sakya in den Fels geschlagen. Im Vordergrund stehen Lehmöfen zum Verbrennen von Duftkräutern. ※ **PAGE DE GAUCHE** Sur la route menant du monastère de Sakya à Lhassa, le Kyichu, au moment de la fonte des neiges, ressemble à un lac aux eaux turquoise. **PAGE DE GAUCHE** la falaise sculptée de Nyethang. **CI-DESSUS** Cette représentation gigantesque du Sakyamuni, le Bouddha historique, a été taillée dans une paroi rocheuse dans le petit village de Nyethang, sur la route de Sakya. Les constructions visibles au premier plan sont des fours en argile dans lesquels on brûle des herbes odorantes.

⁂ **FACING PAGE** a side entrance to the Sakya monastery. view from the courtyard to the three-storeyed entrance of the monastery gate, draped with Tibetan banners. **ABOVE** Nestled in the Gongkar valley, the rooftops of Sakya look out on rugged views of the Khamb La Mountain. ⁂ **LINKE SEITE** ein Seiteneingang ins Kloster Sakya. Blick vom Innenhof auf das dreistöckige Klostertor, das mit tibetischen Bannern behängt ist. **OBEN** Die Dächer des Kloster Sakya schmiegen sich ins Gongkar-Tal; der Blick geht auf den Berg Khamb La. ⁂ **PAGE DE GAUCHE** une entrée latérale du monastère de Sakya. drapée de bannières tibétaines, l'entrée monumentale à deux étages du monastère vue côté cour. **CI-DESSUS** Au cœur de la vallée de Gongkar, Sakya a vue sur les reliefs accidentés du Khamb-La.

※ **FACING PAGE** Monks pose in the exquisitely painted entrance hall of the monastery. frescoes of guardian deities. **ABOVE** oil lamps placed before the image of a goddess in a glass case in the red and gold chapel. **FOLLOWING PAGES** monks during a ceremony in the main hall. ※ **LINKE SEITE** Die Mönche posieren in der großartig ausgemalten Eingangshalle des Klosters. Auf den Fresken sind Schutzgottheiten dargestellt. **OBEN** Öllampen vor der Statue einer Göttin hinter Glas in der rotgoldenen Kapelle. **FOLGENDE DOPPELSEITE** Mönche während einer Zeremonie in der Haupthalle. ※ **PAGE DE GAUCHE** Des moines posent dans le hall d'entrée superbement peint. des fresques représentant des divinités. **CI-DESSUS** Dans la chapelle rouge et or, des lampes à huiles éclairent la statue d'une divinité exposée dans une vitrine. **DOUBLE PAGE SUIVANTE** des moines à l'occasion d'une cérémonie dans le hall principal.

Götz Hagmüller

The Stupa of Bodhnath

Nepal

THE STUPA OF BODHNATH
KATHMANDU

Fluttering flags, prayer wheels, temple bells.

If you ask an average Nepali whether he is Hindu or Buddhist the answer often is "Yes". The two religions are deeply intertwined in the Himalayan kingdom and share similar beliefs, rituals, deities and symbols.

Officially a Hindu kingdom, the river of Buddhism has flowed through Nepal from the earliest times. The birth of the Buddha in about 566 BC took place in an ancient state that is now part of southern Nepal. Some say that buried in the depths of the stupa in Bodnath, one of the largest and oldest in the world, is a relic of the Buddha. Around Bodhnath are numerous Tibetan monasteries, including Shechen, whose abbot, Rabjam Rinpoche, is seen on the facing page. Near Bodhnath is the revered temple of Pashupatinath, dedicated to the Hindu god Shiva. Perched on a hill across town is the equally important stupa of Swayambhunath. Between the gilded spires and white-washed domes of the stupas are painted the all-seeing eyes of the Buddha facing all four directions; the question mark-like "nose" stands for the Nepali numeral "one", a reminder that there is only one true path to nirvana.

Fragt man in Nepal jemand, ob er Hindu oder Buddhist ist, so lautet die Antwort häufig »Ja«. Im Königreich des Himalaja sind die beiden Religionen eng miteinander verwoben und teilen ähnliche Glaubenssätze, Rituale, Gottheiten und Symbole.

Nepal war zwar zunächst ein hinduistisches Königreich, aber der Buddhismus ist hier seit Urzeiten weit verbreitet. Die Geburt Buddhas um 566 v. Chr. ereignete sich in einem Staat auf dem Gebiet des heutigen Südnepal. Der Legende nach liegt in der Tiefe des Stupa von Bodnath, der zu den ältesten der Welt zählt, eine Reliquie Buddhas begraben. In der Umgebung liegen zahlreiche tibetische Klöster, darunter das Kloster Shechen, dessen Abt Rabjam Rinpoche auf der linken Seite zu sehen ist. Unweit von Bodhnath liegt auch der Tempel von Pashupatinath, der der Hindugottheit Shiva geweiht ist. Auf einem Hügel vor der Stadt befindet sich zudem der bedeutende Stupa von Swayambhunath. Zwischen die vergoldeten Spitzen und die weiß getünchten Kuppeln sind die alles sehenden Augen Buddhas gemalt, die in alle vier Himmelsrichtungen blicken. Die dem Fragezeichen ähnliche »Nase« dazwischen ist das nepalesische Schriftzeichen für »Eins« – Mahnung an den einzig wahren Weg zur Erlösung.

Si vous demandez au premier Népalais venu s'il est hindouiste ou bouddhiste, il vous répondra souvent : « Oui ». C'est que les deux religions sont intimement mêlées dans cet Etat himalayen et qu'elles partagent de nombreux rituels, des croyances, des divinités et des symboles.

Si l'hindouisme est la religion officielle de ce royaume, le bouddhisme y est très présent depuis la nuit des temps. En effet, Bouddha est né vers 566 avant notre ère dans un Etat qui fait désormais partie du Népal méridional. Une relique de Bouddha serait même ensevelie dans les profondeurs du stupa de Bodnath, l'un des plus grands au monde. Dans les environs de Bodnath se trouvent de nombreux monastères tibétains, dont celui de Shechen dirigé par Rabjam Rinpoché (page de gauche). Aux abords de Bodnath s'élève le temple de Pashupatinath, dédié à la divinité hindouiste Shiva. Et de l'autre côté de la ville, juché sur une colline, se trouve le stupa tout aussi important de Swayambhunath. Entre les flèches dorées et les dômes peints à la chaux des stupas, rien n'échappe aux yeux de Bouddha tournés vers les quatre points cardinaux. Son nez en forme de point d'interrogation correspond au « 1 » népalais, et nous rappelle qu'une seule voie mène au nirvana.

※ **PREVIOUS PAGES** frescoes of saints in the temple at Shechen monastery. **FACING PAGE** Placed in niches at the base of Bodhnath's dome are deities daubed with vermilion by devotees. **ABOVE** A guardian king astride an elephant near the dome. **BELOW** Prayer flags planted by worshippers at Bodhnath. ※ **VORHERGEHENDE DOPPELSEITE** Heiligenfresken im Tempel des Klosters Shechen. **LINKE SEITE** In den Nischen am Sockel des Stupa von Bodnath stehen Gottheiten, die von den Gläubigen mit zinnoberroter Farbe bemalt wurden. **OBEN** ein Schutzkönig rittlings auf einem Elefanten an der Kuppel. **UNTEN** Gläubige hinterlassen diese Gebetsfahnen in Bodhnath. ※ **DOUBLE PAGE PRECEDENTE** Les fresques du monastère de Shechen représentent des saints. **PAGE DE GAUCHE** Des adeptes ont enduit de vermillon les divinités placées dans des niches au pied du dôme de Bodnath. **CI-DESSUS** un roi gardien sur un éléphant devant le dôme. **CI-DESSOUS** Les fidèles ont planté des drapeaux à prière.

THE TREASURY OF REDISCOVERED
TEACHINGS
VOLUME 31
349
351

⁂ **PREVIOUS PAGES** monks at prayer in the temple of Shechen monastery. A monk's tea bowl and prayer texts. Hanging from the roof are decorative canopies of brocade patchwork. Above the base with the Buddha's all-seeing eyes rises a gilt section of 13 tiers representing the ascent to perfection. At the pinnacle is a parasol, symbol of royalty. **FACING PAGE** The dot between the two eyes represents the Buddha's "third eye" of perception. an image of the founding guru of a Buddhist sect. **ABOVE** a young acolyte at Shechen monastery. The tiger stripes symbolize power. **FOLLOWING PAGES** Hindu deities and Buddhist symbols of snow lions, the eternal knot and the Buddha's all-seeing eyes merge in a decorated gate to Pashupatinath temple. A group of woman devotees in the temple courtyard. ⁂ **VORHERGEHENDE DOPPELSEITEN** betende Mönche im Tempel des Klosters Shechen. die Teeschale und Gebetstexte eines Mönchs. Vom Dach hängen dekorative Baldachine aus buntem Brokat. Über dem Sockel mit den alles sehenden Augen Buddhas ragt ein Abschnitt mit dreizehn Stufen, die das Streben nach Vervollkommnung symbolisieren. An der Spitze ist als Symbol des Königtums ein Sonnenschirm befestigt. **LINKE SEITE** Der Punkt zwischen den beiden Augen repräsentiert Buddhas »drittes Auge« der spirituellen Wahrnehmung. Die Figur des Gründungsgurus einer buddhistischen Sekte. **OBEN** ein junger Novize im Kloster Shechen. Die Tigerstreifen sind ein Symbol für Macht. **FOLGENDE DOPPELSEITEN** Hindu-Gottheiten und buddhistische Symbole von Schneelöwen, dem unendlichen Knoten und dem alles sehenden Buddha vermischen sich an einem verzierten Tor des Pashupatinath-Tempels. eine Gruppe von gläubigen Frauen in einem Innenhof des Tempels. ⁂ **DOUBLES PAGES PRECEDENTES** des moines en prière dans le temple du monastère de Shechen. Les dais en brocart suspendus au plafond ont un rôle décoratif. Le bol à thé d'un moine et des textes de prière. Le socle orné sur ses quatre faces de l'œil du Bouddha est surmonté d'une flèche composée de 13 cercles représentant les 13 degrés de la connaissance. Le parasol planté au pinacle est un symbole de la royauté. **PAGE DE GAUCHE** Le point entre les deux yeux représente le troisième œil du Bouddha, celui de la clairvoyance. Le gourou fondateur d'une secte bouddhiste. **CI-DESSUS** un jeune novice du monastère de Shechen. Les rayures du tigre symbolisent le pouvoir. **DOUBLES PAGES SUIVANTES** Sur ce portail orné du temple de Pashupatinath, des divinités hindouistes côtoient les symboles bouddhiques des lions des neiges, du nœud éternel, et du Bouddha qui voit tout. Un groupe de croyantes dans la cour du temple.

काठमाडौं ३
का. न. प.

Götz Hagmüller Bhaktapur

A medieval traveller's haunt finds a special tenant.

One of the abiding pleasures of the medieval town of Bhaktapur, a short drive east of Kathmandu, is that it is a pedestrian preserve.

Trucks and buses are forbidden inside city limits. Walking its old cobbled streets that link a series of richly-carved temples, shrines and monasteries, dotted in and around great royal squares, is to breathe the syncretic Hindu-Buddhist culture of the Newari people, the earliest settlers of Kathmandu Valley. The town bustles with the life of traditional artisans – potters, woodcarvers and weavers – who display their wares in the open air. Bhaktapur was saved from ruin by an ambitious German-funded urban conservation project in the 1970s. Götz Hagmüller, an Austrian architect, was part of the effort and formed a deep attachment to Bhaktapur. He rented the two upper floors of a *mat*, a rest house for pilgrims. A typical 17th-century Newari building of narrow rooms, pillared verandas and carved windows built around courtyards, it is now Hagmüller's home from home.

Nur eine kurze Fahrstrecke östlich von Kathmandu liegt die mittelalterlichen Stadt Bhaktapur, die zu einer Fußgängerzone deklariert wurde.

Innerhalb der Stadtgrenzen sind LKWs und Busse verboten. Die Straßen mit Kopfsteinpflaster verbinden eine Reihe von Tempeln mit verschwenderischer Holzschnitzerei sowie große königliche Plätze miteinander, wo sich häufig Schreine und Klöster finden. Beim Spaziergang durch diese geschichtsträchtige Stadt spürt man die synkretistische, hindu-buddhistische Kultur des Newar-Volkes, das als erstes im Kathmandu-Tal siedelte. Im geschäftigen Bhaktapur bieten traditionelle Handwerker – Töpfer, Holzschnitzer und Weber – ihre Ware unter freiem Himmel an. Die Stadt konnte in den 1970er Jahren dank eines ehrgeizigen, aus Deutschland geförderten Projekts vor dem Verfall gerettet werden. Der österreichische Architekt Götz Hagmüller war damals mit von der Partie und entwickelte eine tiefe Zuneigung zu Bhaktapur. Er mietete die beiden obersten Stockwerke eines *mat*, einer Pilgerpension. Das charakteristische, um Innenhöfe herum gebaute Newar-Haus aus dem 17. Jahrhundert ist nun mit seinen engen Räumen, den säulengeschmückten Veranden und den holzgeschnitzten Fenstern Hagmüllers zweite Heimat.

Située à quelques heures de route á l'est de Katmandou, la cité médiévale de Bhaktapur offre un plaisir toujours renouvelé : le piéton y est roi.

La circulation est interdite aux camions et aux bus. Se promener dans ses rues pavées anciennes reliant de somptueux temples, sanctuaires et monastères disséminés dans de superbes parcs royaux, c'est aspirer une bouffée de la civilisation syncrétique hindouiste-bouddhique des Newari, premiers habitants de la vallée de Katmandou. La ville vit au rythme des artisans traditionnels – potiers, ébénistes et tisserands – qui présentent leurs marchandises en plein air. Bhaktapur a été sauvée de la ruine dans les années 1970 par un ambitieux projet de préservation financé par des fonds allemands. Götz Hagmüller, qui a participé à cette action, a conçu un profond attachement pour la ville. Il a loué les deux étages supérieurs d'un *mat*, relais pour voyageurs. Cet édifice newari typique du 17e siècle, caractérisé par des pièces étroites, des vérandas à colonnade, des fenêtres en bois sculpté et des cours intérieures, est maintenant le chez-soi de l'exilé Hagmüller.

※ **FACING PAGE** Lush greenery drapes a garden courtyard. **FACING PAGE AND ABOVE** the main courtyard with saris hung to dry on the elaborately carved woodwork set in brick walls. ※ **LINKE SEITE OBEN** Üppige Pflanzen zieren einen Innenhofgarten. **LINKE SEITE UNTEN UND OBEN** In dem zentralen Innenhof trocknen Saris an den feinen Holzschnitzereien, die in das Mauerwerk integriert sind. ※ **PAGE DE GAUCHE, EN HAUT** La cour-jardin est envahie par la végétation. **EN BAS ET CI-DESSUS** Dans la cour principale, des saris sèchent accrochés aux boiseries très ouvragées qui agrémentent les murs de brique.

※ **PREVIOUS PAGES** the long living room with its open timberwork. **ABOVE** The main seating is a divan placed against slanting windows that give the room privacy. ※ **VORHERGEHENDE DOPPELSEITE** das geräumige Wohnzimmer mit offenem Gebälk. **OBEN** Der große Diwan vor den schrägen Fenstern, die den Raum besonders gemütlich erscheinen lassen, lädt zum Verweilen ein. ※ **DOUBLE PAGE PRECEDENTE** Dans ce salon tout en longueur, la charpente est apparente. **CI-DESSUS** Le divan est adossé à des fenêtres inclinées qui confèrent à la pièce une certaine intimité.

※ **ABOVE** The guest room with its slanted glass-paned windows overlooks the garden. The windows open upwards. **FOLLOWING PAGES** A scalloped "peacock" arch leads into the dining room decorated with well-scrubbed brass dishes for eating and serving. A pergola fashioned from old wooden columns provides shade in the paved garden. ※ **OBEN** Vom Gästezimmer mit den schrägen Fenstern blickt man in den Garten. Die Fenster werden nach oben geöffnet. **FOLGENDE DOPPELSEITEN** Ein muschelförmiger Bogen führt ins Esszimmer, das mit glänzend poliertem Messinggeschirr zum Speisen und Servieren aufwartet. In dem gepflasterten Garten sorgt eine Pergola aus alten Holzsäulen für Schatten. ※ **CI-DESSUS** Cette pièce de réception, également dotée de fenêtres inclinées donne sur le jardin. Les ouvrants des fenêtres se rabattent vers le haut. **DOUBLES PAGES SUIVANTES** La porte de la salle à manger où la vaisselle en cuivre étincelle est surmontée d'un arc polylobé. une pergola faite de colonnes de récupération en bois donne de l'ombre dans le jardin pavé.

Pemayangtse Monastery
Rumtek Monastery
Shiv Niwas Palace
Vijayanagar

india

Pemayangtse Monastery
West Sikkim

Guarded by the Five Treasures of the Great Snow.

Blessed with breathtaking views of the Kanchenjunga, the third highest mountain in the world, the Pemayangtse monastery is the most important of more than a hundred monasteries in India's northeastern state of Sikkim.

Kanchenjunga in Tibetan means "Five Treasures of the Great Snow" and *Pemayangtse* translates as the "Perfect Sublime Lotus". High mountain passes at altitudes of 14, 000 to 18,000 feet link Sikkim to Tibet in the north, Bhutan and Bengal in the south and Nepal in the west. Padmasambhava, the Indian saint who consolidated Tibetan Buddhism, is said to have passed through Sikkim in the eighth century. Until 1975 the state was ruled by a long line of kings, one of whom established Pemayangtse at the turn of the 18th century. The monastery belongs to the Nyingmapa order of Tibetan Buddhism. More than a hundred monks still live here; at several times in the year – including the Sikkimese New Year in February – Pemayangtse resonates with the sound of masked dancers. Thousands of pilgrims come to worship and watch the spectacle.

Das Pemayangtse-Kloster ist das bedeutendste von über hundert Klöstern in Sikkim im Nordosten Indiens. Vom Kloster, dessen Name »Vollkommene Lotusblüte« bedeutet, bietet sich ein atemberaubender Ausblick auf den Kangchendzönga, den dritthöchsten Berg der Welt.

Der tibetische Name des Berges heißt übersetzt »Fünf Schatzkammern des Großen Schnees«. Hochgebirgspässe auf 4000 bis 5500 Metern Höhe verbinden Sikkim im Norden mit Tibet, im Süden mit Bhutan und Bengalen und mit Nepal im Westen. Der indische Heilige Padmasambhava, der den Buddhismus in Tibet begründete, soll im 8. Jahrhundert durch Sikkim gereist sein. Einer der Könige, die bis zum Jahre 1975 das Land über viele Jahrhunderte regierten, gründete an der Wende zum 18. Jahrhundert das Kloster Pemayangtse. Das Kloster, in dem noch über hundert Mönche leben, gehört zum Nyingmapa-Orden des tibetischen Buddhismus. Mehrmals im Jahr, darunter zum sikkimesischen Neujahrsfest im Februar, werden im Kloster Pemayangtse Maskentänze zelebriert, zu denen tausende von Gläubigen und Zuschauern strömen.

Bénéficiant d'une vue imprenable sur le Kangchenjunga, le troisième sommet du monde, le monastère de Pemayangtse est le plus important de la bonne centaine de monastères que compte le Sikkim, Etat du nord-est de l'Union indienne.

En tibétain, *Kangchenjunga* signifie «Cinq Trésors de la Grande Neige» et *Pemayangtse* «Lotus Sublime». Des cols situés à des altitudes allant de 4000 à 5500 mètres relient le Sikkim au Tibet au nord, au Bhoutan et au Bengale au sud, et au Népal à l'ouest. Padmasambhava, le saint d'origine indienne qui a fondé le bouddhisme tibétain, aurait traversé le Sikkim au 8e siècle. Jusqu'en 1975, le pays a été dirigé par une longue dynastie de rois, dont le fondateur de Pemayangtse au début du 18e siècle. Une bonne centaine de moines vivent encore dans ce monastère de l'école bouddhiste tibétaine Nyingma. A plusieurs reprises dans l'année, à commencer par le Nouvel An du Sikkim en février, le monastère vit au rythme de danseurs masqués, spectacle qui attire des milliers de pèlerins.

⁂ **FACING PAGE** The Chinese dragon beneath the brickwork cornice is a symbol of power. acolyte monks who join the monastery at a young age. **ABOVE** Pemayangtse with a spectacular vista of the Kanchenjunga range. **FOLLOWING PAGES** Ornate decorations of flowers, clouds and snow lions on columns and brackets follow a precise Tibetan iconography. The doors painted red are a sign of good fortune. ⁂ **LINKE SEITE** Der chinesische Drache unter dem Backsteinsims gilt als Machtsymbol. Die Novizen treten schon im Kindesalter ins Kloster ein. **OBEN** Pemayangtse mit einem spektakulären Blick auf das Kangchendzönga-Massiv. **FOLGENDE DOPPELSEITE** Die prunkvollen Verzierungen mit Blüten, Wolken und Schneelöwen auf Säulen und Streben richten sich nach einer genau festgelegten tibetischen Ikonographie. Die rot gestrichen Türen sollen Glück bringen. ⁂ **PAGE DE GAUCHE** Le dragon chinois sous la corniche en briquetage est symbole de puissance. Les novices entrent très jeunes au monastère. **CI-DESSUS** Le monastère se détache sur l'arrière-plan spectaculaire du Kangchenjunga. **DOUBLE PAGE SUIVANTE** Les fleurs, nuages et lions des neiges couvrant colonnes et consoles font partie de l'iconographie tibétaine. Le rouge des portes est signe de bonheur.

※ **FACING PAGE** The gate from the entrance steps leads to a richly-frescoed veranda and the main prayer hall. **RIGHT AND BELOW** The repainting and decoration, completed in 2002, is a tribute to surviving artistic skills. ※ **LINKE SEITE** Das Tor an den Eingangsstufen führt zur Hauptgebetshalle und zu einer verschwenderisch mit Fresken verzierten Veranda. **RECHTS UND UNTEN** Die Restaurationsarbeiten durch versierte Handwerker wurden 2002 abgeschlossen. ※ **PAGE DE GAUCHE** Le portillon en haut de l'escalier d'entrée mène à une véranda ornée de fresques somptueuses et à la grande salle de prière. **A DROITE ET CI-DESSOUS** La restauration des peintures et autres éléments décoratifs, achevée en 2002, est un hommage à des traditions artistiques qui se sont perpétuées jusqu'à nos jours.

Rumtek Monastery
East Sikkim

In the land of the orchid and the rhododendron.

Buddhists plant prayer flags in the belief that the wind reads the mantras printed on them and scatters them far and wide, bringing merit to all pilgrim souls, not just a single worshipper.

In the morning mist, the outlines of Rumtek monastery, 24 km from Gangtok, the capital of Sikkim, appear in a forest of prayer flags. Rumtek is the seat of the Kagyu, or Black Hat, order of Tibetan Buddhism. Devotees believe that when the Karmapa Lama, the leader of the Kagyu sect, performs a secret but spiritually powerful ceremony, the Black Hat, said to be made from the hair of angels, soars above his head. The 800-year-old Kagyu lineage is now headed by the seventeenth incarnation of the Karmapa Lama, a young man who fled to India from Tibet in 2000 but is yet to be formally installed at Rumtek. The monastery was established in Sikkim in the 16th century but was damaged in an earthquake. An imposing new complex on the lines of the Tsurphu monastery in Tibet was built in the 1960s. The main shrine, monks' quarters, reliquaries, a monastic college and nunnery occupy an entire hillside, integral to the sacred geography of the Himalayas.

Die Buddhisten stellen Gebetsfahnen auf, denn sie glauben, der Winde lese die aufgedruckten Mantras und verstreue sie weit und breit zum Heil – nicht nur des einzelnen Gläubigen, sondern aller pilgernden Seelen.

Das 24 Kilometer von Gangtok, der sikkimesischen Hauptstadt, entfernte Kloster Rumtek erscheint im Morgennebel wie in einem Wald von Gebetsfahnen. Rumtek ist der Sitz des Kagyu-Ordens, auch »Schwarze Hüte« genannt, einem tibetisch-buddhistischen Orden. Seine Anhänger glauben, dass in dem Moment, wenn der Karmapa Lama der Kagyusekte eine geheime, doch spirituell mächtige Zeremonie vollführt, ein schwarzer Hut aus Engelshaar über seinem Kopf schwebt. Als Oberhaupt der 800 Jahre alten Abstammungslinie der Kagyu wird heute die siebzehnte Inkarnation des Karmapa Lama verehrt, ein junger Mann, der im Jahr 2000 aus Indien nach Tibet floh. Offiziell hat er sein Amt in Rumtek allerdings noch nicht angetreten. Das Kloster besteht seit dem 16. Jahrhundert in Sikkim, wurde aber bei einem Erdbeben beschädigt. In den 1960er Jahren wurde das eindrucksvolle heutige Kloster als Replik des Tsurphu-Klosters in Tibet neu errichtet. Insgesamt sind der Hauptschrein, der Wohnbereich der Mönche, Reliquiare, eine Klosterschule und ein Nonnenkloster über einen ganzen Hügel verteilt und fügen sich nahtlos in die heilige Landschaft des Himalaja ein.

Les bouddhistes sont persuadés que le vent lit les mantras qui sont inscrits sur les drapeaux à prière et qu'il les disperse aux quatre vents, dispensant ses bienfaits à toute la communauté de pèlerins.

Dans la brume matinale, la silhouette du monastère de Rumtek, situé à 24 kilomètres de Gangtok, la capitale du Sikkim, s'élève au-dessus d'une forêt de drapeaux de prière. Rumtek est le monastère de l'ordre bouddhiste tibétain de Kagyu, ou Bonnet noir. Les fidèles croient que lorsque leur maître, le lama Karmapa accomplit une cérémonie secrète mais d'une grande force spirituelle, le Bonnet noir, que l'on dit fait de cheveux d'ange, s'élève au-dessus de sa tête. Vieille de 800 ans, la lignée de Kagyu est dirigée à l'heure actuelle par la dix-septième incarnation du lama Karmapa, un jeune tibétain qui s'est réfugié en Inde en l'an 2000 et doit encore être nommé officiellement chef de la communauté de Rumtek. Ce monastère fondé au 16e siècle a été en partie détruit par un tremblement de terre. Dans les années 1960, on a construit un nouveau complexe monumental sur le modèle du monastère de Tsurphu au Tibet. Le sanctuaire principal, les appartements des moines, les reliquaires, le collège monastique et un couvent couvrent tout un versant de colline, se fondant dans la géographie sacrée de l'Himalaya.

* **FACING PAGE** prayer flags with written mantras planted round a container with votive offerings by worshippers. **ABOVE** Rumtek occupies an entire hillside with a series of outbuildings. **BELOW** The monastery looks on to magnificent views of the Kanchenjunga range of the Himalayas. * **LINKE SEITE** Gebetsfahnen mit schriftlichen Mantras an einem Häuschen mit Weiheopfern der Gläubigen. **OBEN** Mit einer Reihe von Nebengebäuden nimmt Rumtek einen ganzen Hügel ein. **UNTEN** Großartiger Ausblick vom Kloster auf das Kangchendzönga-Massiv im Himalaja. * **PAGE DE GAUCHE** Des drapeaux à prière sur lesquels sont inscrits des mantras signalent cette petite construction renfermant des offrandes faites par des fidèles. **CI-DESSUS** Le monastère de Rumtek et ses dépendances couvrent tout un versant de montagne. **CI-DESSOUS** le spectacle magnifique de Kangchenjunga, dans la chaîne de l'Himalaya.

⁂ **FACING PAGE** the main courtyard of Rumtek monastery. **ABOVE AND BELOW** The gate house of Rumtek opening into a walled courtyard with a raised walkway is in the classical style of Tibetan architecture. ⁂ **LINKE SEITE** der zentrale Innenhof des Klosters Rumtek. **OBEN UND UNTEN** Das Torhaus von Rumtek, das in einen ummauerten Hof mit einem erhöhten Gang führt, ist charakteristisch für den klassischen Stil der tibetischen Architektur. ⁂ **PAGE DE GAUCHE** la cour principale du monastère. **CI-DESSUS ET CI-DESSOUS** Le corps de garde donnant sur une cour ceinte de hauts murs et dotée d'un chemin de ronde surélevé est caractéristique de l'architecture tibétaine classique.

⁂ **FACING PAGE AND ABOVE** Rumtek is home to about 200 young monks, of all age-groups, for whom it is a place of work and play. ⁂ **LINKE SEITE UND OBEN** In Rumtek leben etwa 200 Mönche aller Altersstufen, um zu arbeiten und zu spielen. ⁂ **PAGE DE GAUCHE ET CI-DESSUS** Quelque 200 jeunes moines, de tout âge, vivent à Rumtek, s'adonnant au travail et au jeu.

⁂ **ABOVE** The banners shielding the verandas are emblazoned with the symbol of the double thunderbolt that represents the indestructible force of truth. **FACING PAGE** Auspicious snow lions form the capitals of painted columns. ⁂ **OBEN** Die Banner vor den Veranden sind mit dem Symbol des Doppelblitzes verziert, der die unzerstörbare Kraft der Wahrheit symbolisiert. **RECHTE SEITE** Schneelöwen bilden die Kapitelle der bemalten Säulen. ⁂ **CI-DESSUS** les bannières protégeant les vérandas des regards indiscrets sont revêtues du double éclair, symbole de la force indestructible de la vérité. **PAGE DE DROITE** Des lions des neiges de bon augure constituent les chapiteaux de colonnes peintes.

※ **BELOW AND FACING PAGE** Silk curtains and intricate frescoes adorn the monastery's interior in contrast to the impassive symmetry of the exterior. **FOLLOWING PAGES** A massive mural of a guardian king stands sentinel near a hanging shield inside the shrine. A silken tassle hangs from an ornamental doorknob surrounded by a trailing vine of sacred lotus blossoms. ※ **UNTEN UND OREGHTE SEITE** Seidenvorhänge und komplizierte Fresken schmücken das Innere des Klosters – ein Kontrast zu der kargen Symmetrie des äußeren Erscheinungsbilds. **FOLGENDE DOPPELSEITEN** Neben dem abschirmenden Vorhang im Inneren des Schreins hält auf einem mächtigen Wandbild ein Schutzkönig Wache. Eine Seidenquaste hängt an einem verzierten Türknauf, während der Türrahmen mit Ranken heiliger Lotusblüten verziert ist. ※ **CI-DESSOUS ET PAGE DE DROITE** Très richement décoré de tentures de soie et de fresques complexes, l'intérieur du monastère contraste avec la géométrie reposante de l'extérieur. **DOUBLES PAGES SUIVANTES** A l'intérieur du sanctuaire, une peinture murale impressionnante représentant un roi protecteur monte la garde près d'un blason suspendu. Un gland en argent agrémente une poignée de porte décorative cernée par un lotus grimpant sacré en fleur.

Shiv Niwas Palace
Udaipur Rajasthan

The haunt of James Bond
and Bollywood stars.

With palaces of breathtaking beauty built in and around lakes and surrounded by a landscape of rugged hills, Udaipur is among the most romantic cities in Rajasthan.

The Shiv Niwas Palace is the last of a series of magnificent palaces that Udaipur's rulers built from the 16th century onwards on the crest of a hill overlooking Lake Pichola. The present owner Arvind Singh Mewar's great grandfather Fateh Singh commissioned Shiv Niwas as a private residence in the Indo-European style in the early years of the 20th century. It was presented to his father Bhagwat Singh on the occasion of his marriage in 1939 and Arvind Singh grew up here. Later it served as a private guest house before being converted into a hotel in 1978. A new set of guest rooms was added on the upper storey and the swimming pool in the courtyard was enlarged. James Bond paid an extended visit in 1982 for the filming of "Octopussy". The superb wall ornamentation in coloured glass adds to its glittering appeal. It is now a perfect setting for Bollywood stars and the international jet set to stage sumptuous weddings.

Das von zerklüfteten Hügeln umgebene Udaipur mit seinen atemberaubend schönen Palästen auf und an den Seen gilt als eine der außergewöhnlich romantischen Städte in Rajasthan.

Der Shiv-Niwas-Palast wurde von den Herrschern über Udaipur als letzter von mehreren prächtigen Palästen gebaut, die ab dem 16. Jahrhundert auf der Spitze eines Hügels mit Blick auf den Pichola-See errichtet wurden. Anfang des 20. Jahrhunderts gab Fateh Singh, der Großvater des heutigen Besitzers Arvind Singh Mewar, Shiv Niwas als Privatvilla im indo-europäischen Stil in Auftrag. Arvind Singh verbrachte hier seine Kindheit, denn 1939 wurde die Residenz seinem Vater Bhagwat Singh anlässlich seiner Heirat überlassen. Später diente sie als private Gästevilla, bis sie schließlich 1978 in ein Hotel umgebaut wurde. Im oberen Stockwerk wurden mehrere Zimmer hinzugebaut, und der Swimmingpool im Hof wurde vergrößert. 1982 residierte James Bond hier während der Dreharbeiten zu »Octopussy«. Nicht nur die herrlichen Wandornamente aus Buntglas verleihen dem Hotel Glanz und Glitter – ein perfektes Bühnenbild für prächtige Hochzeiten von Bollywood-Stars und Berühmtheiten des internationalen Jetset!

Dans un paysage remarquable, Udaipur, qui s'enorgueillit de palais d'une beauté renversante s'élevant sur des îles lacustres ou sur les rives de lacs, est l'une des villes romantiques du Rajasthan.

Le Shiv Niwas est le dernier en date des palais magnifiques que les souverains de Udaipur ont construit à partir du 16e siècle sur la crête d'une colline surplombant le lac Pichola. Fateh Singh avait fait construire le Shiv Niwas dans le style indo-européen en vogue au début du 20e siècle et avait offert cette résidence privée en cadeau de mariage à Bhagwat Singh, son fils, en 1939. Son petit-fils Arvind Singh Mewar, l'actuel propriétaire, y a passé son enfance. La résidence a par la suite servi de pension privée avant d'être transformée en hôtel en 1978. A cet effet, de nouvelles chambres ont été créées à l'étage supérieur et la piscine dans la cour a été agrandie. James Bond alias Roger Moore y a séjourné longuement en 1982 pour le tournage du film «Octopussy». La superbe décoration murale en verre de couleur ajoute à son lustre. C'est pour les stars de Bollywood et la jet-set internationale l'endroit parfait où fêter des mariages somptueux.

⁂ **PREVIOUS PAGES, CLOCKWISE FROM TOP LEFT** view of the Lake Palace Hotel on an island from the roof terrace of the Shiv Niwas Palace. The central fountain court at Shiv Niwas Palace. The swimming pool, originally a small circular pool, was enlarged when Shiv Niwas was converted into a hotel in 1978. A pattern of lotus flowers in honey-coloured Jaisalmer stone inlay was added during the extension. **ABOVE** a swimming pool in the ruler's private apartment. **RIGHT** the entrance gate to Shiv Niwas in intricately-carved black stone from Dungarpur. **FACING PAGE** The former drawing room, with a cornice and balcony embellished with patterns in blue and pink glass, is now the hotel bar. ⁂ **VORHERGEHENDE DOPPELSEITE, IM UHRZEIGERSINN VON LINKS OBEN** Blick von der Dachterrasse des Shiv Niwas Palace auf das Lake Palace Insel-Hotel. Der zentrale Innenhof des Shiv Niwas Palace mit Springbrunnen. Der ehemals kleine runde Swimmingpool wurde vergrößert, als Shiv Niwas 1978 in ein Hotel verwandelt wurde. Im Zuge des Ausbaus wurde dieses Lotusblütenmuster als Einlegearbeit aus dem Sandstein der Stadt Jaisalmer hinzugefügt. **OBEN** der Swimmingpool im Privatgemach des Herrschers. **RECHTS** Die bildhauerische Ornamentik am Eingangstor zum Shiv Niwas ist aus dem dunklen bläulich schimmernden Stein, für den die Stadt Dungarpur berühmt ist. **RECHTE SEITE** Der ehemalige Salon, dessen Gesims und Balkon mit einem Muster aus blauem und rosafarbenem Glas geschmückt sind, dient heute als Hotelbar. ⁂ **DOUBLE PAGE PRECEDENTE, DANS LE SENS DES AIGUILLES D'UNE MONTRE, À PARTIR D'EN HAUT À GAUCHE** le Lake Palace Hotel vu de la terrasse panoramique du Shiv Niwas Palace. la cour centrale du Shiv Niwas Palace et sa fontaine. La piscine, à l'origine un bassin circulaire, a été agrandie en 1978, à l'occasion de la transformation du Shiv Niwas en hôtel. Le motif de fleurs de lotus en incrustation en pierre de Jaisalmer couleur de miel date aussi de cette époque. **CI-DESSUS** Le souverain disposait d'une piscine dans ses appartements privés. **A DROITE** La pierre noire de Dungarpur de l'entrée monumentale de Shiv Niwas est taillée comme de la dentelle. **PAGE DE DROITE** L'ancien salon, doté d'une corniche et d'un balcon agrémenté d'éléments de verre roses ou bleus, abrite désormais le bar de l'hôtel.

Vijayanagar Hampi
Karnataka

The spellbinding story
of an encounter between gods and kings.

"The king had a thousand elephants with bodies like mountains and miens like demons…the city of Vijayanagar has no equal in the world," wrote Abdul Razzak, a Persian visitor to the court of Devaraya II in 1443. For more than 200 years from the mid-14th century onwards until its decisive sack in 1565, a powerful Hindu empire rose in the Deccan plateau in south India.

The kings of Vijayanagar – City of Victory – were called "rajas". They established a magnificent capital that was also a sacred centre, an invocation to the god Vishnu and his incarnation Rama, the hero of the epic "Ramayana". Great temples and royal palaces went up on the banks of the River Tungabhadra that snakes its way through a mysterious landscape of rising granite rocks that served as natural fortification (following pages). The link between the earthly and the divine conferred a god-like status on the kings; the city grew in the concentric circles of a mandala, a magical diagram representing the universe. Vijayanagar's remains – some preserved, others half-ruined or reduced to rubble – are one of the glories of medieval south Indian architecture.

»Der König besaß tausend Elefanten, deren Leiber waren wie Berge, und ihre Blicke glichen jenen der Dämonen … die Stadt Vijayanagar findet in der Welt nicht ihresgleichen«, so schrieb der Perser Abdul Razzak, der im Jahr 1443 den Hof Devarayas II. besuchte. Ein mächtiges hinduistisches Reich entstand von der Mitte des 14. Jahrhunderts bis zu seinem endgültigen Zusammenbruch 1565 auf dem Dekkan-Plateau in Südindien.

Die Könige von Vijayanagar – der Stadt des Sieges – nannten sich Radschas. Sie gründeten eine prächtige Hauptstadt, die auch als Heiligtum für den Gott Vishnu und seine Inkarnation Rama, den Helden des Ramayana-Epos, fungierte. Am Ufer des Tungabhadra-Flusses, der sich durch eine geheimnisvolle Landschaft mit riesigen Granitfelsblöcken windet – die als natürliche Verteidigungslinie genutzt wurde –, errichteten sie große Tempel und königliche Paläste. Aufgrund der Verbindung von irdischer und göttlicher Macht hatten die Könige einen gottähnlichen Status inne, während sich die Stadt selbst in den konzentrischen Kreisen eines Mandalas, das als magisches Diagramm das Universum repräsentiert, entwickelte. Die erhaltenen, halb verfallenen oder zu Staub gewordenen Überreste von Vijayanagar zeugen vom ruhmvollen Glanz der mittelalterlichen Architektur Südindiens.

«Le roi possédait un millier d'éléphants hauts comme des montagnes et avec des allures de démons… la ville de Vijayanagar n'a pas d'égale au monde», écrivait Abdul Razzak, Persan en ambassade à la cour de Devaraya II en 1443. Pendant plus de deux siècles, à partir du milieu du 14e siècle jusqu'à la mise à sac qui a scellé son destin en 1565, un puissant empire hindou dominait le plateau du Deccan, dans le sud de l'Inde.

Les rois de Vijayanagar – Cité de la victoire – portaient le nom de «radjas». Ils ont fondé une capitale munificente, qui était aussi un centre religieux, dédié au culte de la divinité Vishnou et de son incarnation Rama, héros du poème épique «Ramayana». Des temples imposants et des palais royaux bordaient les rives de la Tungabhadra qui serpente dans un paysage mystérieux d'affleurements de granite qui tenaient de fortification naturelle (double page suivant). Le lien entre le temporel et le spirituel conférait aux rois un statut de quasi-divinité. La ville s'est développée en cercles concentriques rappelant un mandala, diagramme magique qui représente l'univers. L'ancienne Vijayanagar – dont certains édifices ont été conservés et d'autres à moitié détruits ou sont tombés en ruine – est l'une des gloires de l'architecture médiévale du sud de l'Inde.

※ **PREVIOUS PAGES, CLOCKWISE FROM TOP LEFT** view from an arcaded enclosure of elephants' stables facing a royal parade ground. The outstanding 16th-century Vithala Temple. Stone procecсional chariots for deities. The richly carved Ramachandra Temple. **BOTTOM** Carved from granite, the sculpture was once embellished in rich colours. ※ **VORHERGEHENDE DOPPELSEITE, IM UHRZEIGERSINN VON OBEN LINKS** Blick von der säulengeschmückten Einfriedung der Elefantenställe hinter dem königlichen Paradeplatz. DerVishnu geweihte Vithala-Tempel aus dem 16. Jahrhundert. In Stein gegossene Reittiere für die Prozession der Gottheiten. Der mit Skulpturen geschmückte Ramachandra-Tempel, das Hauptheiligtum von Vijayanagar. **UNTEN** Die aus Granit geschlagenen Skulpturen waren früher bunt bemalt. ※ **DOUBLE PAGE PRECEDENTE, DANS LE SENS DES AIGUILLES D'UNE MONTRE, À PARTIR D'EN HAUT À GAUCHE** De ces arcades, on aperçoit les écuries pour éléphants. Le temple de Vithala construit au 16e siècle. Ce temple évoque les processions en l'honneur des divinités du temple de Vithala. Le temple de Ramachandra, constituait le centre religieux de Vijayanagar. **EN BAS** Taillées dans du granite, les sculptures étaient autrefois parées de couleurs.

⁕ **CLOCKWISE FROM TOP LEFT** Images of Rama and the god Krishna, both believed to be reincarnations of the god Vishnu. Sacred images of the bull Nandi, the mount of the god Shiva. Monkeys run wild among the ruins of Vijayanagar and are revered as descendants of the monkey god Hanuman. Friezes of courtly processions and military campaigns on the walls of Vijayanagar's temples. ⁕ **IM UHRZEIGERSINN VON OBEN LINKS** Heilige Statuen des Stiers Nandi, dem Reittier des Gottes Shiva. Wilde, als Abkömmlinge des Affengottes Hanuman verehrte Affenhorden laufen in den Ruinen von Vijayanagar umher. Friese mit höfischen Prozessionen und Kampfhandlungen an den Tempelwänden. Figuren des Helden Rama und des Gottes Krishna, die beide als Reinkarnationen des Gottes Vishnu gelten. ⁕ **DANS LE SENS DES AIGUILLES D'UNE MONTRE, À PARTIR D'EN HAUT À GAUCHE** des statues du taureau sacré Nandi, monture de Shiva. Des hordes de singes, vénérés comme des descendants du dieu-singe Hanuman, déambulent dans les ruines de Vijayanagar. Des scènes de processions et de bataille sur les murs des temples de Vijayanagar. Représentations du héros Rama et du dieu Krishna, considérés comme des réincarnations du dieu Vishnou.

Padmanabhapuram Palace Nagercoil Tamil Nadu

Here, Vishnu's preserving radience fills the universe.

Padmanabhapuram Palace is one of the most outstanding wooden buildings in India, an architectural feat by the master carpenters of Kerala.

Built largely in the 18th century by Martanda Varma, ruler of Travancore, the terracotta tiled roofs and gleaming black plaster floors offset its superb woodwork of polished teak. The royal family moved to Trivandrum in 1790 and henceforth it was only used as summer residence. It may be one good reason why it has survived in such good condition. Although built by a great dynasty of Kerala, a shift in boundaries now locates it just over the border in the state of Tamil Nadu. The palace derives its name from the worship of the god Vishnu, the Preserver of the Universe in the Hindu pantheon. Among Vishnu's manifestations is an image of him reclining on a serpent, with the god Brahma, the Creator, seated on a lotus growing out of his navel. *Padma* in Sanskrit is lotus; *nabha* means navel. Padmanabhapuram is thus the citadel of Vishnu from whose navel emerges the lotus and whose preserving radiance fills the universe.

Padmanabhapuram Palace, ein Meisterwerk der Schreiner aus Kerala, ist ein herausragendes Beispiel der indischen Holzarchitektur.

Der Palast wurde weitgehend im 18. Jahrhundert unter Martanda Varma, dem Herrscher über Travancore, erbaut. Das Dach aus Terrakottaziegeln und die glänzend schwarzen Gipsböden heben sich von dem prächtigen Schnitzwerk in poliertem Teakholz ab. 1790 zog die königliche Familie nach Trivandrum und nutzte den Palast fortan als Sommerresidenz – daher vielleicht blieb er so gut erhalten. Das Bauwerk wurde von einer mächtigen Dynastie in Kerala erbaut, doch haben sich die Grenzen inzwischen so verschoben, dass es heute im Bundesstaat Tamil Nadu liegt. Sein Name leitet sich von der Verehrung des Gottes Vishnu ab, der im hinduistischen Pantheon die ewige Ordnung des Universums aufrechterhält. Hier ist Vishnu als liegende Figur auf einer Schlange abgebildet, während der Schöpfergott Brahma auf einem Lotus sitzt, der aus seinem Nabel wächst. Die Wörter *padma* und *nabha* bedeuten Lotus und Nabel. Padmanabhapuram ist dementsprechend die Zitadelle Vishnus, aus dessen Nabel der Lotus wächst und dessen bewahrendes Strahlen das Universum erfüllt.

Le palais de Padmanabhapuram est un des exemples d'architecture en bois les plus spectaculaires d'Inde. On doit cette prouesse architecturale aux maîtres charpentiers de Kerala.

Construit en grande partie au 18e siècle par Martanda Varma, qui régnait sur le Travancore, le palais présente des toits en tuiles de terre cuite et des sols de calcaire noir luisant, qui surpassent en beauté ses superbes boiseries en teck poli. La famille royale ayant fait de Trivandrum sa capitale en 1790, ce palais est devenu une simple résidence d'été, ce qui explique sans doute pourquoi il est encore en si bon état. Bien qu'il doive sa construction à une grande dynastie du Kerala, un déplacement des frontières a fait qu'il est maintenant situé de l'autre côté de la frontière, dans l'Etat de Tamil Nadu. Le palais tient son nom de la vénération du dieu Vishnou qui est parfois représenté reposant sur un serpent, aux côtés de Brahma, le dieu créateur, assis sur un lotus surgi du nombril de Vishnou. En sanscrit, *padma* signifie lotus et *nabha* nombril. Padmanabhapuram est ainsi la citadelle de Vishnou dont le nombril donne naissance au lotus et dont l'aura protectrice emplit l'univers.

⁕ **ABOVE** a private bathing tank for members of the royal family. The sharply sloping roof shades a stairway into the water. **FACING PAGE** Carved stone pillars adorn the dance hall with its polished black floor of lime plaster. a traditional Kerala bed placed in one of the many palace corridors. ⁕ **OBEN** ein privates Schwimmbecken für die königliche Familie. Im Schatten des steil abfallenden Daches führt eine Treppe zum Wasser. **RECHTE SEITE** Verzierte Steinsäulen schmücken den Tanzsaal mit dem schwarz polierten Boden aus Gipskalk. Ein traditionelles Bett aus Kerala steht in einem der vielen Gänge. ⁕ **CI-DESSUS** Ce bain était réservé aux membres de la famille royale. Le toit très pentu protège du soleil l'escalier descendant dans l'eau. **PAGE DE DROITE** Des piliers sculptés dans la pierre ornent la salle de danse au sol de calcaire noir poli. Ce lit traditionnel du Kerala trône dans un des nombreux corridors du palais.

⁎ **ABOVE** The carved ceiling is upheld by ribbed rafters. The outward-sloping slatted windows help to keep out the harsh sunlight and modulate the circulation of air. **RIGHT** The shape of the staircase parapet is said to be inspired by an elephant's trunk. **FACING PAGE** The coloured glass panes and furniture in the audience chamber were introduced with the arrival of European style. ⁎ **OBEN** Die holzgeschnitzte Decke wird von Rippenbalken gestützt. Die nach außen gewölbten, mit Leisten versehenen Fenster halten das grelle Sonnenlicht ab und regulieren den Luftaustausch. **RECHTS** Ein Elefantenrüssel diente vermutlich als Inspiration für den Entwurf des Treppengeländers. **RECHTE SEITE** Die Buntglasfenster und die Möbel im Audienzzimmer verdanken sich dem frühen europäischen Einfluss. ⁎ **CI-DESSUS** Le plafond en bois sculpté est supporté par des chevrons travaillés. Les jalousies inclinées préservent de la brûlure du soleil et permettent l'aération. **À DROITE** La main courante de l'escalier est censée représenter une trompe d'éléphant. **PAGE DE DROITE** Les vitrages de couleur et le mobilier de la salle d'audience datent de l'arrivée des Européens.

Joerg Drechsel Cochin

Kerala

A landmark church revived as a cultural melting-pot.

With its lagoons, dolphin-filled bays and spice-laden bazaars, Cochin is the most fascinating of cities.

The product of India's long encounter with Europe, a medieval church, a synagogue and the tomb of the Portuguese explorer Vasco da Gama are clustered around the historic Fort Cochin area. For Joerg Drechsel, a German-born exhibition designer, Cochin was the place of childhood fantasy when he first visited Kerala in the early 1970s. Over the years it has become his home. Together with his wife Txuku Iriarte, who is Basque, he spent four years transforming the Malabar House, an 18th-century mansion, into the finest small hotel in Fort Cochin. For years Joerg and Txuku had eyed the parsonage of St Francis Church, a famous landmark occupied by the English painter Anthony Fry. When Fry moved out in 2001, the Bishop agreed to let them have it, provided they undertook a careful restoration of the austere Dutch colonial building. With the welcoming cut-out of Gandhi that he found in a warehouse and select objects, Joerg Drechsel triumphantly captures some of Cochin's cultural diversity.

Cochin ist eine außerordentlich faszinierende Stadt – mit Lagunen, Buchten voller Delfinen und duftenden Gewürzbasaren.

Auf der Insel mit der historischen Festung Cochin finden sich beredte Zeugnisse europäischer Begegnungen mit Indien: die mittelalterliche Kirche, die Synagoge und der Grabstein des portugiesischen Entdeckers Vasco da Gama. Bereits Anfang der 1970er Jahre entdeckte der deutschstämmige Ausstellungsdesigner Joerg Drechsel bei seinem ersten Besuch in Cochin die Stadt seiner Kindheitsfantasien. Inzwischen ist er hier zu Hause und hat mit seiner baskischen Frau Txuku Inarte in vierjähriger Arbeit das Herrenhaus »Malabar House« aus dem 18. Jahrhundert in das feinste kleine Hotel auf Fort Cochin verwandelt. Joerg und Txuku hatten schon vor Jahren ein Auge auf das Pfarrhaus der St.-Francis-Kirche geworfen – einem berühmten Wahrzeichen der Insel, in dem jedoch der englische Maler Anthony Fry wohnte. Als Fry 2001 auszog, überließ der Bischof ihnen das nüchterne holländische Kolonialhaus mit der Auflage, es sorgsam zu restaurieren. Mit dem Konterfei des gastfreundlichen Gandhi, den Joerg Drechsel in einem Lagerhaus entdeckte, und anderen ausgewählten Objekten heißt er seine Besucher in einer Atmosphäre willkommen, die Cochins kulturelle Vielfalt widerspiegelt.

Avec ses lagons, ses baies grouillant de dauphins et des bazars regorgeant d'épices, Cochin est la plus fascinante des villes.

Fruits des influences européennes, une église médiévale, une synagogue et la tombe de l'explorateur portugais Marco Polo sont regroupées autour du site historique de Fort Cochin. Cochin a nourri l'imagination enfantine de Joerg Drechsel, scénographe d'origine allemande, qui a fait sa première visite au Kerala au début des années 1970. Au bout de quatre ans de travaux, son épouse, la Basquaise Txuku Iriarte, et lui-même ont fait de cette demeure du 18e siècle «Malabar House», le plus bel hôtel de charme de Fort Cochin. Depuis des années, Joerg et Tsuku avaient des vues sur le presbytère de l'église St Francis Church, un édifice remarquable, habité par le peintre britannique Anthony Fry. Quand Fry a quitté les lieux en 2001, l'évêque a accepté qu'ils s'y installent, à condition qu'ils restaurent avec soin cette austère construction érigée par les colons hollandais. Avec le Gandhi de carton trouvé dans une grande surface, qui réserve un accueil chaleureux aux visiteurs, et des objets choisis, Joerg Drechsel a su capter avec bonheur certaines facettes de la diversité culturelle de Cochin.

※ **ABOVE LEFT** the entrance to the parsonage leading to the main hall. **ABOVE RIGHT** three traditional masks from north Kerala, for warding off evil spirits, and a planter's chair form a counterpoint in the hall. **BELOW** The dining table with a stone top was made from steel pipes. Against the wall is a tribal sculpture from Karnataka flanked by carved wooden panels from the Deccan. **FACING PAGE** a passage to the bedroom is painted in bright pigments. The wooden images are from north Kerala. ※ **OBEN** Der Eingang des Pfarrhauses führt in die große Halle. In der Halle bilden drei traditionelle Masken aus Nordkerala, die böse Geister abhalten sollen, einen Kontrapunkt zu einem Kolonialstuhl. **UNTEN** Der Esstisch mit einer Steinplatte wurde aus Stahlrohr gefertigt. An der Wand lehnt eine Stammesskulptur aus Karnataka, rechts und links davon stehen geschnitzte Holztafeln vom Dekkan-Plateau. **RECHTE SEITE** Der Gang zum Schlafzimmer ist in leuchtend-satten Farben gestrichen. Die Holzfiguren stammen aus dem Norden Keralas. ※ **CI-DESSUS, À GAUCHE** l'entrée du presbytère, avec la salle principale à l'arrière-plan. **À DROITE** Trois masques rituels du Kerala destinés à protéger des mauvais esprits et une chaise de style colonial forment un contraste saisissant dans cette pièce. **CI-DESSOUS** La table est constituée d'un plateau en pierre reposant sur des tuyaux en acier. Sur le mur du fond, une sculpture tribale du Karnataka est flanquée de panneaux en bois sculptés provenant du Deccan. **PAGE DE DROITE** Le passage menant à la chambre a été peint avec des pigments très lumineux. Les bois sculptés viennent du nord du Kerala.

Nikki Harrison
Illuketia
Apa Villa
Number Eighty-Seven
A Garden Called Brief

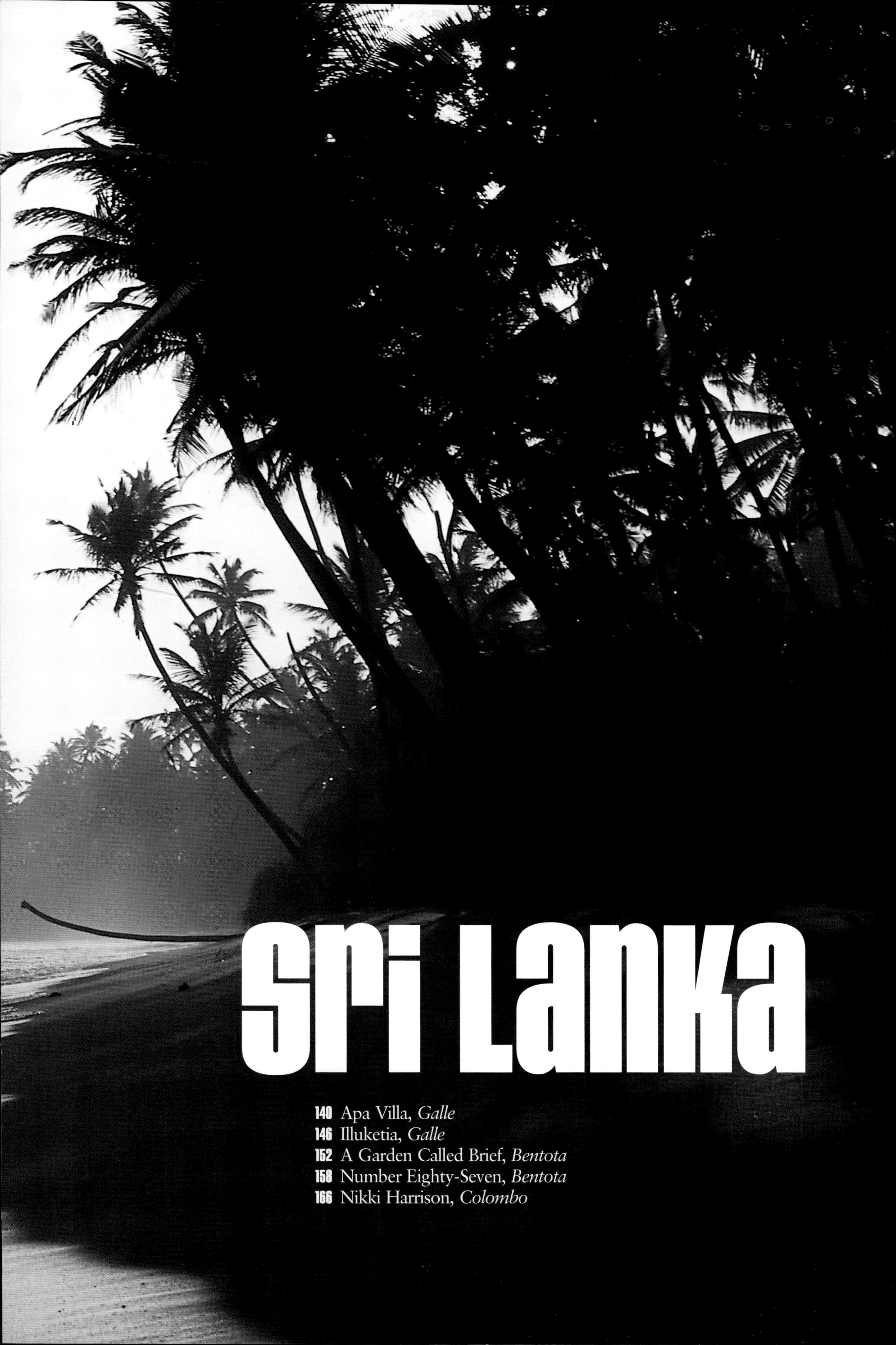

Sri Lanka

Apa Villa Galle

On the rising tide in the Indian Ocean.

Apa is an all-purpose Indonesian word that can mean "how", "why" "what" or "when". When German-born photographer, graphic designer and printer Hans Höfer produced his first guide book to Bali more than thirty years ago it seemed an apt name for his publishing company.

Höfer first visited Sri Lanka twelve years ago and loved it so much that he was soon on a property hunt. Apa was the obvious choice of name for the old guest house he bought on a clear stretch of beach at Thalpe, a few miles south of Galle. After renovation and landscaping, Apa Villa has grown into a series of three ocean-front villas called "Cinnamon", "Cardamom" and "Saffron". Beyond an inner courtyard framed by coconut pillars is the library of the original house and, beyond that, a picture postcard frame of waving palms and the Indian Ocean. The centre piece of the property is the much-copied swimming pool made of concrete. Between running his business in Singapore and an organic farm in Nepal, Höfer's favourite plaything is a 65-foot yacht called Rising Tide.

Apa ist ein allgegenwärtiges Wort in Indonesien, denn es kann »wie«, »warum«, »was« oder »wann« bedeuten. Als der deutschstämmige Fotograf, Grafikdesigner und Drucker Hans Höfer vor über dreißig Jahren seinen ersten Reiseführer über Bali veröffentlichte, schien es ihm als Name für seinen neu gegründeten Verlag überaus passend.

Als Höfer vor zwölf Jahren erstmals nach Sri Lanka kam, war er so begeistert von dem Land, dass er sich direkt auf die Suche nach geeigneten Immobilien machte. Für die alte Pension, die er an einem unbebauten Sandstrand in Thalpe wenige Kilometer südlich von Galle erwarb, kam natürlich kein anderer Name als eben Apa in Frage. Nachdem die Anlage ausgiebig renoviert und gartenarchitektonisch gestaltet wurde, besteht Apa Villa jetzt aus drei Villen mit Meerblick namens »Zimt«, »Kardamom« und »Safran«. Hinter dem mit Säulen aus Kokosholz geschmückten Innenhof liegt die ehemalige Bibliothek des ursprünglichen Hauses mit einem Postkartenblick auf sich wiegende Palmen und den Indischen Ozean. Im Mittelpunkt der Anlage liegt der häufig nachgeahmte Swimmingpool aus Beton. Höfer, der in Singapur Geschäfte macht und in Nepal einen Bio-Bauernhof betreibt, entspannt sich am liebsten auf seiner 20-Meter-Yacht »Rising Tide«.

Apa est un mot indonésien bien utile puisqu'il signifie « comment », « pourquoi », « quoi » ou « quand ». Quand le photographe, graphiste et imprimeur d'origine allemande Hans Höfer a lancé son premier guide sur Bali il y a une bonne trentaine d'années, Apa lui a semblé le nom idéal pour sa maison d'édition.

Lors de sa première visite au Sri Lanka au début des années 1990, Höfer a été à ce point conquis par le pays qu'il s'est rapidement mis en quête d'une propriété. Apa est le nom qui s'est imposé à lui pour l'ancienne pension qu'il a achetée dans la longue baie de Thalpe, à quelques kilomètres au sud de Galle. A l'issue de travaux de rénovation et d'aménagement paysager, Apa Villa a grandi : elle comprend désormais trois bungalows sur le front de mer portant les noms parfumés de « Cinnamon » (cannelle), « Cardamon » (cardamome) et « Saffron » (safran). Une fois passé une cour intérieure encadrée par des colonnes en bois de cocotier, on traverse la bibliothèque de la maison d'origine pour se retrouver face à une vue de carte postale : une plage de palmiers ondoyants sur fond d'océan Indien. La pièce maîtresse de la propriété est la piscine en béton, souvent plagiée. Hans Höfer consacre les heures de loisir que lui laisse la gestion d'une affaire à Singapour et d'une ferme biologique au Népal à son jouet préféré, un yacht de près de 20 mètres de long appelé « Rising Tide ».

* **FACING PAGE** a fishing pontoon from Jaffna converted into a daybed. The 60-foot swimming pool is made entirely from concrete. **ABOVE** The property is on a clear stretch of beach along the Indian Ocean. **FOLLOWING PAGES** The stainless steel dining chairs with teak slats were inspired by a Geoffrey Bawa design. In the courtyard of the villa, stone slabs lead across a black fish pond through the gate onto the pool and the beach. The daybeds in the library are also made of concrete. * **LINKE SEITE** Ein Fischerkahn aus Jaffna wurde in ein Ruhebett verwandelt. Der 18 Meter lange Swimmingpool besteht nur aus Beton. **OBEN** Die Anlage liegt an einem feinsandigen Strand am Indischen Ozean. **FOLGENDE DOPPELSEITE** Die Esszimmerstühle aus Edelstahl mit Teakholzleisten sind einem Design von Geoffrey Bawa nachempfunden. Im Innenhof der Villa führen Steinplatten über einen schwarzen Fischteich durch das Tor hinaus zum Pool und zum Strand. Die Ruhebetten in der Bibliothek sind ebenfalls aus Beton. * **PAGE DE GAUCHE** Une barque de pêcheur provenant de Jaffna est devenue un lit de repos. La piscine longue de 18 mètres est entièrement en béton. **CI-DESSUS** La propriété n'est séparée de l'océan Indien que par une vaste étendue de sable. **DOUBLES PAGES SUIVANTES** Les chaises de salle à manger en inox et lattes de teck sont inspirées d'un design de Geoffrey Bawa. Dans la cour intérieure, des dalles conduisent à la piscine et à la plage, en passant par la porte au-dessus d'un vivier noir. Les lits de repos de la bibliothèque sont aussi en béton.

ILLUKETIA GALLE

A tea planter's bungalow in a garden of rare medicinal plants.

Moving inland from Galle, through picturesque villages set in a luxuriant tropical landscape, one enters a series of low-lying tea estates and rubber plantations.

Although the finest teas are grown in the hills of central Sri Lanka, tea from low-lying areas has a distinctive flavour and is much prized in the Middle East. Near the village of Wanchawala are the gardens of Illuketia. The name derives from a reed-like grass called *illuk*, commonly used as roof thatch, but the soil at Illuketia is doubly blessed. Early in the 19th century it was recorded as a place where rare medicinal plants were grown. Illuketia estate had shrunk to seven acres when Hans Höfer bought it and the old plantation house on a hill was beyond repair. Over the last ten years he has virtually rebuilt it, expanding and renovating to create a boutique hotel. Deep verandas on three sides slope down to swards of lawn, herb gardens, paddy fields, lotus pools and untamed jungle. Surrounding Illuketia for miles are tea plantations that produce Sri Lanka's famous flavour.

Landeinwärts von Galle liegen hinter malerischen Dörfern Tee- und Kautschukplantagen in einer üppigen Tropenlandschaft.

Die feinsten Teesorten werden zwar im zentralen Bergland von Sri Lanka angebaut, aber auch der Tee aus diesen niedrigeren Lagen ist wegen seines besonderen Geschmacks in Asien sehr beliebt. Unweit des Dorfes Wanchawala liegen die Gärten von Illuketia, so genannt in Anlehnung an das schilfähnliche Gras, *illuk*, mit dem Dächer gedeckt werden. Illuketia war im 19. Jahrhundert zudem für den Anbau seltener Arzneipflanzen bekannt. Das Anwesen war auf drei Hektar geschrumpft, als Hans Höfer es erwarb, und die alte Residenz der Plantage war völlig verfallen. Im Laufe der letzten zehn Jahren errichtete er sie von Grund auf neu und erweiterte die Villa zu einem exquisiten Hotel. An drei Seiten neigen sich tief gelegte Veranden über Rasenflächen, Kräutergärten, Reisfelder, Lotusteiche und wilden Dschungel. Rund um Illuketia erstrecken sich kilometerweit die Teefelder, auf denen Sri Lankas einzigartige Teesorten produziert werden.

L'arrière-pays de Galle abrite des villages pittoresques dans une végétation tropicale luxuriante, parmi des plantations d'hévéas et de thé.

Bien que les meilleurs thés soient cultivés dans les montagnes du centre du pays, le thé provenant des zones de basse altitude a une saveur particulière et est très apprécié au Moyen-Orient. Près du village de Wanchawala se trouvent les jardins d'Illuketia, ainsi nommés d'après l'*illuk*, une herbe rappelant le roseau qu'on utilise comme chaume. La terre d'Illuketia est doublement bénie. Au début du 19e siècle, on a constaté que des herbes médicinales rares y poussaient. Lorsque Hans Höfer a acheté Illuketia, la propriété ne s'étendait plus que sur trois hectares et la vieille maison de planteur juchée sur une colline était complètement délabrée. Au cours des dix dernières années, il l'a reconstruite et agrandie pour créer un hôtel de charme. Des vérandas profondes sur trois côtés de la maison donnent sur des pelouses, des jardins simples, des rizières, des bassins recouverts de lotus et sur la jungle. Autour d'Illuketia s'étendent à perte de vue des plantations qui produisent le célèbre thé de Ceylan.

⁂ **PREVIOUS PAGES** The Pond House, a recently-constructed suite, is set at the edge of the lotus pool. **ABOVE** light streams through the metal pyramid roof of the outdoor bathroom. **BELOW** water gushing from the courtyard pool into a granite urn. **FACING PAGE** yellow and olive green cushions on a hand-painted bedspread in the bedroom. ⁂ **VORHERGEHENDE DOPPELSEITE** Die erst kürzlich erbaute Zwei-Zimmer-Suite »Pond House« liegt am Lotusblütenteich. **OBEN** Das Licht fällt durch das pyramidenförmige Metalldach des Freiluft-Badezimmers. **UNTEN** Das Wasser aus dem Swimmingpool im Innenhof sprudelt in ein Granitbecken. **RECHTE SEITE** Kissen in Gelb und Olivgrün auf einer handbemalten Tagesdecke im Schlafzimmer. ⁂ **DOUBLE PAGE PRÉCÉDENTE** « The Pond House », suite de deux pièces de construction récente, s'élève au bord du bassin aux lotus. **CI-DESSUS** Dans la salle de bains de plein air, la lumière filtre par la toiture pyramidale. **CI-DESSOUS** L'eau du bassin de la cour tombe en cascade dans une vasque en granite. **PAGE DE DROITE** Des coussins agrémentent un dessus de lit peint à la main.

A Garden Called Brief

Bentota

A case of sibling revelry between Bevis and Geoffrey Bawa.

No account of 20th-century architecture can be complete without the doffing of caps in the direction of the Sri Lankan architect Geoffrey Bawa.

"Ceylonese" is probably the word he would have preferred. Along with his brother Bevis, older by ten years, Geoffrey formed a bridge between the dying colonial order and the emerging sensibilities of Asian independence. Born of old Burgher stock, in the years 1909 and 1919 respectively, the Bawa brothers grew up in a snobbish world of rambling Colombo mansions, upcountry estates, European education and an undying addiction to Rolls Royce cars. But they knew that their allegiance lay in the magical landscape and Buddhist heritage of the Isle of Serendip. Bevis Bawa acquired the rubber plantation called "Brief" – named after the proceeds of one legal brief handled by his lawyer father – outside Bentota in 1929. Here he established a garden that became the precursor to Geoffrey's famous landscape overlooking a lagoon at Lunuganga. Bevis Bawa died in 1993. Geoffrey, who continued to create buildings from a wheelchair, died after a ten-year gap in 2003. Both brothers have left an indelible impression on the map of modern Sri Lanka.

An dem singhalesischen Baumeister Geoffrey Bawa kommt keine Architekturgeschichte des 20. Jahrhunderts vorbei.

Wahrscheinlich hätte ihm die Bezeichnung »ceylonesisch« besser gefallen, denn gemeinsam mit seinem zehn Jahre älteren Bruder Bevis verkörperte er die Verbindung zwischen der schwindenden Kolonialordnung und den neuen Empfindlichkeiten asiatischer Unabhängigkeit. Die 1909 und 1919 geborenen Brüder wuchsen in einer alten Burgher-Familie holländischer Kolonialherren auf und bewegten sich in der snobistischen Welt weitläufiger Herrenhäuser in Colombo, mit Grundbesitz im Hochland, Ausbildung in Europa und einer unstillbaren Leidenschaft für Rolls-Royces. Dennoch fühlten sie sich der zauberhaften Landschaft und dem buddhistischen Erbe der ehrwürdigen Insel Serendip verbunden. 1929 kaufte Bevis Bawa die Kautschukplantage namens »Brief« vor Bentota, die nach einem juristischen Schriftstück ihres Vaters, einem Anwalt, so genannt wurde. Bevis Bawa legte einen Garten an, der Geoffreys berühmter Gartenanlage über der Lagune von Lunuganga als Vorbild diente. Bevis Bawa starb 1993, und Geoffrey, der noch aus dem Rollstuhl heraus weiterhin Gebäude entwarf, folgte ihm 2003. Die beiden Brüder haben einen einzigartigen Beitrag zur Gestaltung des modernen Sri Lanka geleistet.

Aucun panorama de l'architecture du 20e siècle ne saurait être complet sans un hommage à l'architecte sri lankais Geoffrey Bawa.

Encore qu'il aurait certainement préféré qu'on le qualifie de « ceylanais » car avec son frère aîné Bevis, Geoffrey a jeté un pont entre l'ordre colonial moribond et les sensibilités apparues dans le sillage de l'indépendance des anciennes colonies en Asie. Nés respectivement en 1909 et 1919 d'une vieille famille de Burghers – issus de mariages mixtes entre Hollandais et Cinghalais –, les frères Bawa ont grandi entre des villas construites de manière anarchique à Colombo, des propriétés dans l'arrière-pays, une éducation européenne et une éternelle passion pour les Rolls. Mais ils savaient que leur vie était dans les paysages magiques et l'héritage bouddhique de Serendip, comme l'appelaient les commerçants arabes. En 1929, Bevis Bawa a fait l'acquisition d'une plantation d'hévéas à l'extérieur de Bentota, à laquelle il a donné le nom de « Brief », « affaire » en anglais, par référence à son père avocat. Il y a créé un jardin qui a été le précurseur du célèbre jardin paysagé de Geoffrey qui surplombe un lagon près de Lunuganga. Bevis Bawa est décédé en 1993. Geoffrey, qui a continué à travailler de son fauteuil roulant, est décédé dix ans plus tard, en 2003. Les deux frères ont laissé une marque indélébile sur la carte du Sri Lanka moderne.

⁂ **FACING PAGE** entrance to the Japanese garden. **ABOVE** The wrought iron gates and gateposts capped by sculptures were designed by Bevis Bawa. **BELOW** one of the many secluded resting spots. The water spout and trough are also of Bawa's design. **FOLLOWING PAGES** Lotus-filled water bodies and classical sculptures are focal points in many of the garden rooms. The garden has been left exactly as Bevis Bawa designed it and is open to the public. ⁂ **LINKE SEITE** Zugang zum Japanischen Garten. **OBEN** Die schmiedeisernen Tore und die Torwächter wurden nach Entwürfen von Bevis Bawa angefertigt. **UNTEN** eine der vielen lauschigen Rückzugsmöglichkeiten. Der Wasserspeier und der Trog wurden ebenfalls von Bevis Bawa entworfen. **FOLGENDE DOPPELSEITE** Wasserspiele mit Lotusblüten sowie klassische Skulpturen sind unverkennbare Bestandteile der Gartenanlage. Der öffentlich zugängliche Garten blieb genau so erhalten, wie Bevis Bawa ihn gestaltet hat. ⁂ **PAGE DE GAUCHE** l'entrée du jardin japonais. **CI-DESSUS** Les portails en fer forgé surmontés de sculptures ont été dessinés par Bewis Bawa. **CI-DESSOUS** L'un des nombreux endroits retirés où l'on peut se reposer. La gargouille et la vasque sont aussi des créations de Bawa. **DOUBLE PAGE SUIVANTE** Des plans d'eau décorés de fleurs de lotus et de sculptures classiques sont les vedettes de bien des chambres de verdure. Le jardin, resté tel que Bevis Bawa l'avait conçu, est maintenant ouvert au public.

Number Eighty-Seven
Bentota

The wilderness of Geoffrey Bawa's private garden.

During the 1960s and 1970s architect Geoffrey Bawa was at the height of his powers. Between designing a host of public buildings, from Sri Lanka's parliament to a major university and a series of private houses and hotels for the country's political elite, he longed to indulge in the preservation of small, intimate ruins.

Bawa was a trained architect and lawyer and never lost the chance to importunate rich or artistic friends to buy properties. He persuaded the Italian sculptor Lidia Duchini, married to a Sri Lankan, to buy two early 18th-century houses sloping towards marshland near the busy coastal road from Colombo to Galle. The plot was called "Number Eighty-Seven", a name that has stuck. Bawa created a series of terraced water bodies and pavilions filled with the murmur of the sea. In 1996 Rohan and Dulanjalee Jayakody bought and lovingly restored the private wilderness. Dulanjalee is the daughter of assassinated Sri Lankan premier Ranasinghe Premadasa; Rohan, an art collector and pioneer of floriculture in Sri Lanka, was a friend and admirer of Geoffrey Bawa's. "Number Eighty-Seven" is their homage to Bawa's genius.

In den 1960er und 1970er Jahre lag die Glanzzeit des Architekten Geoffrey Bawa. Während eine Reihe öffentlicher Gebäude, wie das Parlament Sri Lankas und eine bedeutende Universität, sowie zahlreiche Privathäuser und Hotels nach seinen Entwürfen gebaut wurden, galt sein wahres Interesse dem Wiederaufbau kleiner ausgesuchter Ruinen.

Bawa war als Architekt und Anwalt gleichermaßen erfahren und drängte seine Künstlerfreunde gern zum Kauf von Immobilien. Er überredete die italienische Bildhauerin Lidia Duchini, Gattin eines Singhalesen, zum Erwerb zweier Häuser aus dem 18. Jahrhundert, die unweit der viel befahrenen Küstenstraße von Colombo nach Galle abschüssig zum Sumpfland lagen. Das Grundstück war als »Number Eighty Seven« ausgezeichnet, was als Name hängen blieb. Bawa entwarf mehrere Wasser führende Elemente und Pavillons, die vom Klang des Meeresrauschens erfüllt sind. 1996 ging diese Dschungellandschaft in den Besitz von Rohan und Dulanjalee Jayakody über, die sie liebevoll in Stand setzten. Dulanjalees Vater war der ermordete Premierminister Sri Lankas, Ranasinghe Premadasa, während Rohan, Kunstsammler und Pionier singhalesischer Blumenzucht, ein Freund und Bewunderer Geoffrey Bawas war. Das Ehepaar betrachtet »Number Eighty-Seven« als persönliche Hommage an das Genie Bawas.

Les années 1960 et 1970 ont été les plus fécondes pour l'architecte Geoffrey Bawa. Entre la conception d'une kyrielle d'édifices publics, du parlement national à une grande université, et des maisons particulières et hôtels pour l'élite politique du pays, il s'est surtout intéressé à la restauration de modestes constructions de charme.

Architecte et avocat de formation, Bawa n'a jamais manqué une occasion de travailler au corps ses amis artistes ou fortunés pour qu'ils investissent dans la pierre. C'est ainsi qu'il a persuadé la sculptrice italienne Lidia Duchini, mariée à un Sri Lankais, d'acheter deux maisons du début du 18e siècle surplombant un terrain marécageux à proximité de la route côtière très fréquentée qui relie Colombo à Galle. La parcelle s'appelait « Number Eighty Seven » (Numéro Quatre-vingt-sept), et le nom lui est resté. Bawa y a créé une série de plans d'eau étagés et de pavillons qu'emplit le murmure de la mer. En 1996, Rohan et Dulanjalee Jayakody ont acheté cette propriété perdue dans la jungle et l'ont restaurée avec amour. Dulanjalee est la fille de Ranasinghe Premadasa, Premier ministre sri lankais assassiné ; Rohan, collectionneur d'art et pionnier de la floriculture au Sri Lanka, était un ami et admirateur de Geoffrey Bawa. « Number Eighty-Seven » est un hommage au génie de ce dernier.

* **PREVIOUS PAGES, CLOCKWISE FROM TOP LEFT** a granite grinding wheel in a garden courtyard. The stairs lead to a secluded lap pool that Rohan Jayakody added after acquiring the property. a stone image of Ganesh, the elephant-headed Hindu god, placed by the terrace steps. Sections of one old house were removed and carefully reassembled to create a garden folly. **FACING PAGE** A staircase was added to replace a steep ladder to the floor above. A traditional oil lamp hangs above the dining table. **ABOVE** Planter's chairs and benches line the pillared veranda. **FOLLOWING PAGES** Rows of Buddhas and stupas in tiers at the Gangaramaya temple near Beira Lake in Colombo. On the lake itself is the Seema Malakaya temple designed by Geoffrey Bawa. * **VORHERGEHENDE DOPPELSEITE, IM UHRZEIGERSINN VON OBEN LINKS** ein Mahlstein aus Granit in einem bepflanzten Innenhof. Die Treppe führt zu einem abgelegenen Swimmingpool, den Rohan Jayakody nachträglich hinzufügte. Teile eines alten Hauses wurden abgetragen und sorgfältig zu einem markanten Gartenensemble arrangiert. Skulptur des elefantenköpfigen Hindugottes Ganesh an der Terrassentreppe. **LINKE SEITE** Die ehemalige steile Leiter ins Obergeschoss wurde durch diese Treppe ersetzt. Über dem Esstisch hängt eine traditionelle Öllampe. **OBEN** Kolonialmöbel auf der säulengeschmückten Veranda. **FOLGENDE DOPPELSEITE** Mehrere Reihen mit Buddhastatuen und Stupas im Gangaramaya-Tempel unweit des Beira-Sees in Colombo. Direkt am See liegt der von Geoffrey Bawa entworfene Seema-Malakaya-Tempel. * **DOUBLE PAGE PRECEDENTE, DANS LE SENS DES AIGUILLES D'UNE MONTRE, À PARTIR D'EN HAUT À GAUCHE** une meule en granite, élément crnemental du jardin. La volée de marches conduit à un bassin peu profond, à l'abri des regards, que Rohan a fait construire. Une vieille maison a été partiellement démontée et soigneusement remontée pour créer une folie. Une statue en pierre de Ganesh, la divinité hindouiste à tête d'éléphant, monte la garde au pied de l'escalier de la terrasse. **PAGE DE GAUCHE** Un escalier est venu remplacer une échelle raide par laquelle on accédait à l'étage supérieur. Une lampe à huile traditionnelle éclaire la table de la salle à manger. **CI-DESSUS** Des sièges et des bancs de style colonial invitent au repos sur la véranda à colonnade. **DOUBLE PAGE SUIVANTE** Le temple de Gangarama, sur les rives du lac Beira, à Colombo, est célèbre pour sa composition étagée de bouddhas et de *stupas*. Au milieu du lac s'élève le temple de Seema Malaka, conçu par Geoffrey Bawa.

Nikki Harrison Colombo

Light, white and bright.

Nikki Harrison has been a mistress of many trades. She has worked as a fashion designer, youth counsellor, school headmistress and PR consultant. No role has fitted her better than taking up designing interiors and managing hotels in Sri Lanka.

She arrived from England more than two decades ago as an expatriate wife and stayed on. Her home, a colonial bungalow that she found some years ago, still retained old wooden-blade ceiling fans and a floor of Burma teak in the living room. What Nikki calls "a little tender loving care" was actually a painstaking exercise in removing layers of varnish, opening out the dining room and converting a disused breakfast room into a sleek terrazzo-tiled kitchen. Taking her cue from the lightness of colonial houses, she painted the red concrete floors white, stripped the unusual curved staircase of its handrail and removed wood paneling from the walls. Filling the house with objects collected over the years and furniture designed locally, she has brought back the graceful elegance of its heyday.

Nikki Harrison ist ein Tausendsassa. Sie arbeitete als Modedesignerin, Jugendberaterin, Schulrektorin sowie in der Werbung. Der krönende Höhepunkt aber dieser Karrieren lag in dem Entschluss, als Innenarchitektin und Hotelmanagerin in Sri Lanka tätig zu werden.

Als Frau eines Ausländers wanderte sie vor 20 Jahren aus England ein und blieb. Als sie ihr jetziges Haus entdeckte, fand sie darin noch Deckenventilatoren mit Drehflügeln aus Holz sowie einen Holzboden aus birmanischem Teak im Wohnzimmer. Es kostete einige Mühe, zahlreiche Lackschichten zu entfernen, das Wohnzimmer zu vergrößern und einen ungenutzten Frühstücksraum in eine schnittige Küche mit Terrazzoboden zu verwandeln. Aber Nikki bezeichnet diese Anstrengungen lächelnd als »zärtlichen Liebesdienst«. Sie ließ sich von den hellen Kolonialbauten inspirieren und strich die roten Betonböden weiß. Außerdem entfernte sie das Geländer der ungewöhnlich gewundenen Treppe und die Holzvertäfelung von den Wänden. Indem sie das Haus mit Möbeln aus der Umgebung sowie den vielen kleinen Kostbarkeiten dekorierte, die sie über die Jahre gesammelt hat, gab sie ihm seine ursprüngliche Anmut und Eleganz zurück.

Nikki Harrison a exercé avec brio bien des métiers : créatrice de mode, conseillère d'orientation, directrice d'école et consultante en relations publiques. Mais elle a tout bonnement excellé dans celui d'architecte d'intérieur et de directrice d'hôtels au Sri Lanka.

Il y a une bonne vingtaine d'années, elle a quitté l'Angleterre pour suivre son mari et elle est restée au Sri Lanka. Sa maison, un bungalow de style colonial trouvé il y a quelques années, était encore équipée de ventilateurs à pales de bois fixés au plafond et dotée d'un parquet en teck birman dans le salon. Ce que Nikki appelle «aimer d'amour tendre» fut en fait un travail minutieux : elle a décapé les boiseries, ouvert la salle à manger et transformé la salle de petit-déjeuner tombée en déshérence en cuisine dépouillée pourvue d'un sol en terrazzo. Trouvant son inspiration dans la légèreté des maisons coloniales, elle a peint en blanc les sols de béton rouges, débarrassé de sa main courante l'escalier faisant un virage inhabituel et arraché les lambris. Avec des objets collectionnés au fil des ans et du mobilier créé sur place, elle a rendu à la maison l'élégance de ses beaux jours.

⁕ **FACING PAGE** Alcoves under the staircase were created by removing old wooden panelling. The two statues are wooden cores of old Buddha images. Old green-painted cupboards add colour to the gleaming white kitchen with stainless steel fittings. **ABOVE** The veranda upstairs serves as a living area for the bedrooms. The buffalo head on the table is partly made of wood and was found in an antique dealer's yard. ⁕ **LINKE SEITE** Nachdem die alte Holzvertäfelung entfernt wurde, entstanden diese Nischen unter der Treppe. Die beiden Statuen bestehen aus dem hölzernen Kern alter Buddhafiguren. Die alten grün gestrichenen Schränke setzen farbliche Akzente in der strahlend weißen Edelstahlküche. **OBEN** Die Veranda im Obergeschoss schließt sich als Wohnzimmer ans Schlafzimmer an. Die Eigentümerin erwarb den teilweise aus Holz gefertigten Büffelschädel auf dem Tisch von einem Antiquitätenhändler. ⁕ **PAGE DE GAUCHE** Nikki Harrison a ménagé des niches sous l'escalier en enlevant les vieux lambris. Les deux statues sont des armatures en bois d'anciennes statues de Bouddha. Des buffets anciens peints en vert mettent une touche de couleur dans la cuisine d'un blanc étincelant aux accessoires en inox. **CI-DESSUS** A l'étage supérieur, la véranda sert de salon commun aux chambres. Nikki Harrison a trouvé chez un antiquaire la tête de buffle complétée par des pièces en bois qui trône sur la table.

House on the Lake
Jürgen von Jordan
Bagan Hotel

Myanmar

Bagan Hotel
Bagan

The call of Buddhism.

Cradled by the grand sweep of the Ayeyarwady River, the view across the plain of Bagan with its thousands of pagodas, one red-brick Buddhist temple after another, with the occasional white-washed or golden spire reaching heavenwards, is one of the heart-stopping sights of Asia.

About a decade after ascending the throne of Bagan in 1044, King Anawrahta was converted to Therawada Buddhism by a young monk. Enthralled by the rationalism of the new doctrine, he embarked on its spread among his people, replacing it with forms of animist worship that existed earlier. Some 13,000 pagodas were built between 1057 and 1287, when Bagan was invaded by Kublai Khan's army. More than 2000 remain today, many of them covered with frescoes and images of the Buddha. There are so many pagodas in Bagan that two, in fact, are within the tree-shaded garden of the Bagan Hotel. Overlooking the river, the hotel was rebuilt in 1997 by Myanmar's leading architect U Myint Han, and commands a superb location in the old town.

Atemberaubend ist die Aussicht am großen Bogen des Ayeyarwady-Flusses – und eine der schönsten Asiens. Der Blick schweift über das Hochland von Bagan mit tausenden von Pagoden und buddhistischen Tempeln in rotem Backstein sowie hier und da einem weiß gewaschenen oder goldenen Turm, der in den Himmel strebt.

Ein junger Mönch überzeugte König Anawrahta zehn Jahre nach seiner Krönung in Bagan im Jahr 1044 davon, zum Theravada-Buddhismus zu konvertieren. Der König war vom Rationalismus der neuen Lehre so begeistert, dass er sich für ihre Verbreitung im Volk einsetzte und so Formen animistischer Verehrung zurückdrängte. Von 1057 bis 1287 – als das Heer des Großkhan Kubilai Bagan eroberte – wurden 13 000 Pagoden gebaut, von denen 2000 mit Fresken und Bildern des Buddha erhalten blieben. In Bagan gibt es so viele Pagoden, dass schon allein im Baumschatten des Hotels Bagan zwei stehen. Das Hotel mit Blick auf den Fluss und in bester Lage in der Altstadt wurde 1997 von dem führenden birmanischen Architekten U Myint Han wieder aufgebaut.

Lovée dans le vaste lit de l'Irrawaddy, la plaine de Pagan est l'un des paysages les plus saisissants d'Asie, avec ses milliers de pagodes, ses temples bouddhiques se touchant presque et, ça et là, une flèche blanche ou en or, qui part à l'assaut des cieux.

Une dizaine d'années après être monté sur le trône de Pagan en 1044, le roi Anawratha a été converti au bouddhisme theravada par un jeune moine. Séduit par le rationalisme de cette doctrine nouvelle, il a œuvré à sa diffusion parmi ses sujets, l'associant aux cultes animistes pratiqués jusqu'alors. C'est ainsi que 13 000 pagodes ont été construites entre 1057 et 1287, année de la prise de Pagan par les armées de Kubilaï Khan. Il en subsiste plus de 2 000, ornées pour certaines de fresques et de représentations du Bouddha. Deux des innombrables pagodes de Pagan se trouvent précisément dans le jardin ombragé du Bagan Hotel. Cet établissement dominant le fleuve et la vieille ville a été reconstruit en 1997 par l'architecte national vedette, U Myint Han.

❊ **PREVIOUS PAGES** Golden stupas and gilded images of the Buddha adorn many of the pagodas scattered in the riverside plain of Bagan. **ABOVE** votive terracotta urns in the garden of the Bagan Hotel. **FACING PAGE** an ancient brick pagoda and glazed Burmese jars near the hotel's swimming pool. ❊ **VORHERGEHENDE DOPPELSEITE** Goldene Stupas und vergoldete Buddhadarstellungen schmücken viele der Pagoden, die man verstreut im flussnahen Hochland von Bagan findet. **OBEN** Votivurnen aus Terrakotta im Garten des Hotel Bagan. **RECHTE SEITE** eine alte Pagode aus Backstein und glasierte birmanische Übertöpfe am Swimmingpool des Hotels. ❊ **DOUBLE PAGE PRECEDENTE** Des stupas et des bouddhas dorés ornent nombre des pagodes qui émaillent la plaine fluviale de Pagan. **CI-DESSUS** des urnes votives en terre cuite dans le jardin du Bagan Hotel. **PAGE DE DROITE** près de la piscine de l'hôtel, une pagode ancienne en briques et des jarres vernissées birmanes.

Jürgen von Jordan Bagan

A private sunset garden.

Jürgen von Jordan grew up in the countryside around the Bavarian Alps. Much of his working life was spent in Bangkok, running a company that sold heavy machinery.

Business first took him to Yangon in 1970 and from that visit he was bewitched by Myanmar. For Von Jordan, as the cliché goes, there was no looking back. In 1991, many inhabitants of the old town were shifted to a wasteland called New Bagan. Fearing the presence of "bad spirits" many residents refused to move. In partnership with a Burmese friend, Von Jordan bought a plot cheaply by the Ayeyarwady River and landscaped a garden. The original bamboo house with verandas on three sides was extended with a new structure in teak. He found gifted local masons and carpenters to create his "sunset garden". Since 1995, Von Jordan has run a charitable foundation from here that supports a series of village schools, orphanages and provincial hospitals. He lives here in the dry winter months, enjoying his "quiet refuge in a little-known paradise".

Jürgen von Jordan wuchs in den Bayrischen Alpen auf. In Bangkok leitete er lange Jahre ein Unternehmen für Maschineneinrichtung.

Seit seiner ersten Geschäftsreise nach Yangon im Jahr 1970 ist er von Myanmar geradezu verzaubert. Es gab schlichtweg keinen Weg zurück. 1991 sollten viele Bewohner der Altstadt in eine Einöde namens Neu-Bagan umgesiedelt werden. Viele Menschen fürchteten jedoch böse Geister und weigerten sich umzuziehen. Gemeinsam mit einem birmanischen Freund kaufte von Jordan ein preiswertes Grundstück am Ayeyarwady-Fluss und legte dort einen Garten an. Das vorhandene Bambushaus mit Veranden an drei Seiten wurde um einen Neubau aus Teak erweitert. Der Besitzer beauftragte talentierte ortsansässige Maurer und Schreiner mit der Gestaltung seines »Gartens des Sonnenuntergangs«. Von diesem Domizil aus leitet von Jordan seit 1995 eine gemeinnützige Stiftung, die Dorfschulen, Waisen- und Krankenhäuser in der Provinz unterstützt. In den trockenen Wintermonaten genießt er hier sein »stilles Refugium in einem Paradies, das nur wenige kennen«.

Jürgen von Jordan, originaire des Alpes bavaroises, a passé la majeure partie de sa vie active à la tête d'une entreprise spécialisée dans la vente d'équipements lourds.

Ses affaires l'ont amené à Yangon, qui s'appelait alors Rangoon, en 1970. Il est aussitôt tombé sous le charme du Myanmar et, comme c'est très souvent le cas, n'a jamais envisagé de retour en arrière. En 1991, de nombreux habitants de la vieille ville ont été déplacés vers les terres en friche de la Nouvelle Pagan, mais ils refusaient souvent de s'y installer à cause des «esprits malveillants» qui pourraient y rôder. Avec un ami birman, von Jordan a ainsi pu acheter pour une bouchée de pain une propriété sur les rives de l'Irrawaddy. Il a chargé d'excellents ouvriers et artisans locaux d'agrandir le bâtiment d'origine en bambou doté de vérandas sur trois côtés en lui adjoignant une construction en teck, et de créer un «jardin du coucher de soleil». Depuis 1995, la maison héberge les bureaux de l'association caritative dirigée par von Jordan, association qui apporte son soutien financier à divers orphelinats, écoles de village et hôpitaux provinciaux. Von Jordan vit ici pendant les mois secs d'hiver, profitant de son «refuge tranquille dans un paradis méconnu».

⁜ **FACING PAGE** Teak posts support the stairways and roof. A Burmese puppet of a horse hangs in the veranda. **ABOVE** The veranda is the main living area, designed as part of the garden. ⁜ **LINKE SEITE** Teakholzpfosten stützen die Treppe und das Dach. Eine birmanische Pferdemarionette hängt auf der Veranda. **OBEN** Im Grunde findet das Leben auf der Veranda statt, die in den Garten integriert ist. ⁜ **PAGE DE GAUCHE** Des poteaux de teck soutiennent l'escalier et le toit. une marionnette birmane suspendue au plafond de la véranda. **CI-DESSUS** Conçue comme partie du jardin, la véranda est la pièce principale.

HOUSE ON THE LAKE
INLE LAKE

A unique way of life.

When the mists come rolling down the nearby mountains, the flat, shallow expanse of Inle Lake is wrapped in mystery. Here the Intha tribe – *intha* means "sons of the lake" – have evolved an aquatic culture uniquely their own.

They build homes on stilts and cultivate floating vegetable gardens, developed from a combination of silt and tangled growths of water hyacinth. The main form of transport is boat; Intha fishermen propel their canoes by twisting a leg around a single oar. They are a prosperous, industrious people: farming, fishing, weaving, cheroot-making and metalwork are common occupations. In the village of In-Chan, U San Khin and Daw Kyin Mee, left, live in an old house. Their only son died of jaundice leaving behind a widow and son; his photographs are among their treasured memories. For generations the family owned rice paddies in the area. But the landholding has diminished and yields have shrunk. The quiet simplicity of their home holds a mirror to the dignified survival of a remarkable culture.

Der Nebel aus den nahen Bergen legt sich wie ein geheimnisvoller Schleier auf die ausgedehnte Fläche des Inle-Sees. Der Stamm der Intha – *intha* bedeutet »Söhne des Wassers« – hat hier eine einzigartige Wasserkultur geschaffen.

Sie wohnen in Pfahlbauten und bauen Gemüse in schwimmenden Gärten an, die sie aus einer Mischung aus Schlick und ineinander verschlungenen Wasserhyazinthen herstellen. Boote dienen als Haupttransportmittel, und die Inthafischer betätigen das Ruder ihres Kanus, indem sie ein Bein darum schlingen. Die Wirtschaft dieses wohlhabenden, fleißigen Volkes umfasst Ackerbau, Fischerei, Weberei, Metallarbeiten sowie die Herstellung von Zigarillos. U San Khin und Daw Kyin Mee wohnen in einem alten Haus im Dorf In-Chan. Ihr einziger Sohn starb an Gelbsucht und hinterließ eine Frau und einen Sohn – Fotos halten die Erinnerung an sie lebendig. Seit Generationen besitzt die Familie Reisfelder in der Gegend, aber der Grundbesitz hat sich vermindert, und auch die Erträge wurden geringer. Die stille Einfachheit ihres Hauses spiegelt das würdevolle Überleben einer bemerkenswerten Kultur wider.

Lorsque les brumes dévalent les pentes des montagnes voisines, les eaux étendues et peu profondes du lac Inle sont enveloppées de mystère. Les Inthas («fils du lac») vivent ici dans des maisons sur pilotis.

Les Inthas pratiquent des cultures maraîchères uniques en leur genre sur des jardins flottants – en fait de larges bandes de jacinthes d'eau et autres herbes aquatiques qu'ils ont recouvertes de boue et de terre avant de les ensemencer. Les pêcheurs se déplacent surtout en canoë, et ont une manière bien à eux de manœuvrer en enroulant une jambe autour de la rame. Les Inthas sont un peuple travailleur et prospère qui tire le gros de ses revenus de l'agriculture, de la pêche, du tissage, de la fabrication de cigarillos et du travail des métaux. U San Khin et Daw Kyin Mee (page de gauche) habitent une vieille maison dans le village de In-Cahn. Leurs souvenirs les plus chers sont les photographies faites par leur fils aîné décédé de la jaunisse, laissant une veuve et un enfant. Cette famille de riziculteurs depuis des générations a vu ses terres rétrécir et ses revenus diminuer. La simplicité paisible de leur foyer renvoie l'image de la survivance dans la dignité d'une civilisation remarquable.

※ **FACING PAGE** Vegetable gardens cover parts of Inle Lake where the Intha built homes on stilts. A teak staircase leads to the two-storeyed house. **ABOVE** A covered wooden bridge links settlements on the lake. ※ **LINKE SEITE** In der Nähe der Intha-Pfahlbauten ist der Inle-See häufig mit schwimmenden Gemüsegärten bepflanzt. Eine Treppe aus Teakholz führt zu dem zweistöckigen Haus. **OBEN** Eine überdachte Holzbrücke verbindet die Siedlungen am See. ※ **PAGE DE GAUCHE** Les cultures maraîchères recouvrent une partie du lac Inle sur lequel les Inthas ont construit des maisons sur pilotis. l'escalier en teck de la maison à deux étages. **CI-DESSUS** Un pont de bois couvert relie entre elles les maisons du lac.

※ **FACING PAGE AND ABOVE** Wooden shelving, glazed terra cotta urns for drinking water and split bamboo baskets are used for storage in the kitchen. The coal stove is on a platform to reduce the risk of fire in a wooden house. **FOLLOWING PAGES** A glass-fronted teak cabinet in the main room stores valuables including lacquer dishes and clothes. ※ **LINKE SEITE UND OBEN** Die Holzregale, Trinkgefäße aus glasierter Terrakotta und Bambuskörbe in der Küche dienen der Lagerung. Der Kohleofen steht erhöht, um das Brandrisiko in dem Holzhaus zu verringern. **FOLGENDE DOPPELSEITE** Der Vitrinenschrank aus Teak im Hauptraum enthält die Wertsachen, darunter Kleidung und Lackgeschirr. ※ **PAGE DE GAUCHE ET CI-DESSUS** Dans la cuisine, les denrées sont stockées sur des étagères en bois, dans des urnes en terre cuite et des paniers en bambou fendu. Le poêle à charbon est surélevé pour limiter les risques d'incendie. **DOUBLE PAGE SUIVANTE** Dans la pièce principale, les objets de valeur – des plats en laque aux vêtements – sont rangés dans une vitrine en teck.

※ **ABOVE** Kerosene lanterns are the main form of lighting after dark. **BELOW** A mosquito net drapes the sleeping area on the wooden floor. **FACING PAGE** Large metal trunks are used for storing clothes and bed linen keeping them safe from termites. ※ **OBEN** Nach Einbruch der Dunkelheit sind Kerosinlampen die Hauptlichtquelle. **UNTEN** Ein Moskitonetz ist über dem Schlafplatz gespannt. **RECHTE SEITE** In großen Metalltruhen sind Kleidung und Bettwäsche sicher vor Termiten. ※ **CI-DESSUS** Des lampes à pétrole constituent le principal éclairage à la nuit tombée. **CI-DESSOUS** Une moustiquaire protège le lit posé à même le plancher. **PAGE DE DROITE** Les vêtements et le linge de maison sont rangés dans de gros coffres en métal, à l'abri des termites.

Inle Princess Resort

Inle Lake

A precious family legacy.

Misuu Borit tells the story of the Inle Princess Resort with candour and charm:

When she was small her father ran a small guest-house in Nyaung Shwe village on Inle Lake. He dreamed of a foreign education for his daughter and hoped that one day she would help him build a professional hotel owned and managed by a local family that would be a symbol of pride for the Shan people. Parental aspiration has been happily rewarded. Misuu returned with both an education and a European husband. In Magyizin village, on the eastern shore of the lake, they built the resort in 1996, basing the design on traditional Intha and Shan architecture. Almost everything in the resort, with its 46 chalets, from the fabrics to the furniture, is indigenous and of their own devising. Misuu and Yannick Borit also produce pottery and hand-made paper on the 20-acre property surrounded by tranquil views of rice fields on the water. The resort acquired its name because Misuu's father always referred to her as "my little princess".

Offen und charmant erzählt Misuu Borit die Geschichte des Inle Princess Resort:

In ihrer Kindheit leitete der Vater eine kleine Pension im Dorf Nyaung Shwe am Inle-See. Er träumte davon, seiner Tochter eine Erziehung im Ausland zu ermöglichen – in der Hoffnung, dass sie ihm eines Tages bei der Errichtung eines professionell geführten Hotels helfen würde, das, als Symbol für den Stolz des Shan-Volkes, in der Hand von Einheimischen liegen und auch von ihnen geführt werden sollte. Der väterliche Ehrgeiz wurde mehr als belohnt: Misuu kehrte mit einer Ausbildung und einem europäischen Ehemann zurück. Am östlichen Seeufer erbauten sie 1996 im Dorf Magyizin das Resort im Stil der traditionellen Architektur der Shan und Intha. In der 46 Chalets umfassenden Anlage wurde beinahe alles von ihnen selbst entworfen und von Einheimischen hergestellt – von den Stoffen bis zu den Möbeln. Misuu und Yannick Borit produzieren auf dem zehn Hektar großen Gelände überdies Keramik und handgeschöpftes Papier. Die Anlage inmitten von Reisfeldern verdankt ihren Namen der Tatsache, dass Misuus Vater seine Tochter stets »kleine Prinzessin« nannte.

Misuu Borit raconte avec beaucoup de candeur et de charme:

Quand elle était petite, son père dirigeait une petite pension de famille dans le village de Nyaung Shwe, sur le lac Inle. Il rêvait de voir sa fille faire des études à l'étranger et espérait qu'un jour elle l'aiderait à monter un hôtel digne de ce nom. Cet établissement serait entre les mains d'une famille locale qui serait la fierté du peuple Shan. Et ce rêve s'est réalisé: Misuu est revenue au pays, diplôme en poche, avec un mari européen. C'est à Magyizin, un village de la rive est du lac, que Misuu et son mari ont construit le complexe en 1996, s'inspirant de l'architecture traditionnelle intha et shan. Dans cet ensemble de 46 bungalows, le couple a presque tout conçu lui-même, des tissus au mobilier, à partir de matériaux locaux. Misuu et Yannick Borit fabriquent aussi de la poterie et du papier artisanal sur cette propriété de 10 hectares située au milieu d'un cadre paisible de rizières inondées. En souvenir de son père qui l'appelait souvent «ma petite princesse», Misuu a nommé le complexe Inle Princess.

⁂ **PREVIOUS PAGES** Framed by palms and banana trees, the resort's chalets are built in traditional Intha style. **FACING PAGE** The resort's simple interiors were designed by local artisans. Many of the rooms in the resort have private balconies facing the lake. **ABOVE** Fishermen glide by with cone-shaped fishing nets. **FOLLOWING PAGES** Priests and pilgrims make a religious boat trip aboard a traditional royal barge with pagoda roofs and a prow in the shape of a mythical bird. ⁂ **VORHERGEHENDE DOPPELSEITE** Die im traditionellen Stil der Intha erbauten Chalets liegen inmitten von Palmen und Bananenstauden. **LINKE SEITE** Die schlichte Inneneinrichtung des Resorts haben einheimische Handwerker entworfen. Viele Zimmer verfügen über private Balkone mit Blick auf den See. **OBEN** Fischer mit kegelförmigen Netzen gleiten auf dem See vorbei. **FOLGENDE DOPPELSEITE** Priester und Pilger auf einer religiösen Bootsfahrt in einer traditionellen königlichen Barke, deren Bug einem mythischen Vogel nachgestaltet wurde. ⁂ **DOUBLE PAGE PRECEDENTE** dans un décor de palmiers et de bananiers, les bungalows construits dans la tradition intha. **PAGE DE GAUCHE** Les intérieurs simples ont été réalisés par des artisans locaux. La plupart des chambres ont des balcons privés donnant sur le lac. **CI-DESSUS** Un pêcheur équipé d'une nasse conique glisse sur les eaux du lac. **DOUBLE PAGE SUIVANTE** des prêtres et des pélerins en déplacement, sur une barge royale traditionnelle avec des toits en pagode et une proue en forme d'oiseau mythique.

22
8996

A Historic Villa in Mandalay

A poignant period piece.

Descended from the Buddha, the people of Myanmars believe they are the first inhabitants of the world. That is what the word *Myanmar* actually means.

By the mid-19th century however, after a long, often bloody cycle of tribal conflicts, Myanmar was overtaken by the British rulers in neighbouring India. Following two Anglo-Burmese wars, benevolent King Mindon ascended the throne in 1853. Deeply religious yet curious about the outside world, he transferred his capital north, from Amarapura to Mandalay. He began to send young men abroad, among them U Kaung. Queen Victoria received Mindon's envoy in Britain. As a minister, U Kaung was later a key figure in the succession of Thibaw, the last Burmese king. Influenced by what he had seen, U Kaung commissioned a European firm to build a Palladio-inspired mansion in Mandalay. Now an adjunct to a Buddhist monastery, the villa's lavishly-carved doors, passages, classical columns and pedimented windows in teak are a haunting reminder of old Burma's passing infatuation with the West.

Die Birmanen sehen sich als Abkömmlinge Buddhas und glauben, sie seien die ersten Bewohner der Erde gewesen. Das ist die eigentliche Bedeutung des Wortes *Myanmar.*

Mitte des 19. Jahrhunderts eroberten die Briten vom benachbarten Indien aus Myanmar, das auf eine lange blutige Geschichte von Stammeskriegen zurückblickte. Nach zwei britisch-birmanischen Kriegen bestieg der großherzige König Mindon 1853 den Thron. Der tief religiöse Herrscher interessierte sich auch für fremde Länder und verlegte die Hauptstadt von Mandalay ins nördliche Amarapura. Darauf sandte er junge Männer ins Ausland, darunter auch U Kaung, den Königin Victoria als König Mindons Gesandten in London empfing. Unter dem Einfluss seiner Reiseerlebnisse gab U Kaung einem europäischen Unternehmen den Auftrag, in Mandalay ein von Palladio inspiriertes Herrenhaus zu bauen. Die Villa ist heute an ein buddhistisches Kloster angeschlossen, aber die aufwändig geschnitzten Türen, überdachten Gänge, klassischen Säulen und Fenster mit Giebeln aus Teakholz gemahnen an die inzwischen schwindende Anziehungskraft des Westens für das alte Birma.

Descendant du Bouddha, les habitants du Myanmar croient être les premiers habitants du monde, ce que signifie d'ailleurs le nom *Myanmar.*

Au milieu du 19e siècle, les Britanniques, alors souverains aux Indes, ont mis fin aux longues luttes intestines qui avaient souvent laissé le pays exsangue. A l'issue de deux guerres anglo-birmanes, le populaire Mindon est devenu roi de Birmanie en 1853 et a transféré la capitale d'Amapura à Mandalay, plus au nord. Cet homme profondément religieux n'en était pas moins curieux du monde extérieur : il a envoyé de jeunes émissaires à l'étranger, dont U Kaung, qui fut reçu par la reine Victoria. Devenu ministre, U Kaung a par la suite joué un rôle clé dans la succession de Thibaw, le dernier roi birman. Influencé par ce qu'il avait vu à l'étranger, U Kaung a chargé un entrepreneur européen de bâtir une maison de style palladien à Mandalay. Les portes somptueusement sculptées, les circulations, les colonnes d'inspiration classique et les fenêtres en teck à fronton sont autant de détails de cette maison, désormais située dans l'enceinte d'un monastère, qui rappellent de manière obsédante l'engouement passager de l'ancienne Birmanie pour l'Occident.

❊ **PREVIOUS PAGES** doric pillars intersperse with elaborately-carved door panels of Burmese teak. **ABOVE** a double plaster staircase at the entrance to the villa. **RIGHT AND FACING PAGE** Monks from a nearby monastery have made the former minister's villa their own. **FOLLOWING PAGES** novice taking a siesta. ❊ **VORHERGEHENDE DOPPELSEITEN** Dorische Säulen unterbrechen die fein geschnitzten Türfüllungen aus birmanischem Teakholz. **OBEN** eine stuckverzierte Doppeltreppe am Eingang zur Villa. **RECHTS UND RECHTE SEITE** Die Mönche aus dem nahe gelegenen Kloster fühlen sich in der ehemaligen Gesandtenvilla wie zu Hause. **FOLGENDE DOPPELSEITE** Vovize während der Siesta. ❊ **DOUBLE PAGE PRECEDENTE** Des pilastres doriques alternent avec des portes finement sculptées en bois de teck birman. **CI-DESSUS** à l'entrée de la villa, un escalier en plâtre à volée double. **A DROITE ET PAGE DE DROITE** Les moines du monastère voisin ont fait leur cette villa. **DOUBLE PAGE SUIVANTE** novices à l'heure de la sieste.

※ **FACING PAGE AND ABOVE** A spiral teak staircase leads to the gabled villa's roof. The neo-classical rotunda with Corinthian capitals was once the centerpiece leading to the Italianate rooftop. Pedimented windows and a gabled terrace dominate the villa's façade. **FOLLOWING PAGES** a richly-carved transom above ornate doors. the spiral staircase leading to the roof. ※ **LINKE SEITE** Über eine Wendeltreppe aus Teakholz gelangt man zum Giebeldach der Villa. Die neoklassische Rotunde mit korinthischen Kapitellen fungierte einst als Mittelstück, das zu dem Dach in italienischem Stil führte. Giebelfenster und eine Terrasse mit Giebel zieren die Fassade der Villa. **FOLGENDE DOPPELSEITE** ein aufwändig geschnitzter Türsturz über prunkvoll verzierten Türen. Die Wendeltreppe zum Dach. ※ **PAGE DE GAUCHE** l'arrivée sous les combles de l'escalier en teck. Cette rotonde néoclassique dotée de chapiteaux corinthiens menait autrefois au toit italianisant. La façade est marquée par des fenêtres à fronton et une terrasse à pignons. **DOUBLE PAGE SUIVANTE** une imposte délicatement ouvragée domine une porte richement ornée. Départ de l'escalier en spirale menant aux combles.

Chulathat Kitibutr
Vip's Villa
Swairiang Guesthouse
Rolf and Helen von Bueren
A Rice Barge

THAILAND

Sri's Garden House
The Maha Bhetra
A Private Holiday Villa
Jean-Michel and Patsri Beurdeley

VIP'S VILLA CHIANG MAI

A healing garden for the senses.

A fragrant jasmine-like flower, the *kaew* is often grown in Thailand as a hedge. In season, the white blossoms fill the northern hill town of Chiang Mai with a heady scent.

Suan Kaew means the "Garden of Kaew Flowers". It is the name of a village about 15 miles north of Chiang Mai. It was here that Vibhanand Rangsit – Vip for short – stumbled upon a plot of land amidst rice paddies and wooded hills. He commissioned an architect friend, Archarn Dulphichai, and landscape designer Patraporn Charusorn, who happens to be a cousin, to build him a traditional house in a garden setting. Vip had the foresight not to interfere with their design. With its steeply-pitched roof, the house came up amidst bamboo groves and layered plantings of foliage and flowering plants. Vip works part of the week as an acupuncturist in Bangkok. But Vip's Villa has now grown into a guest house around the garden (following pages). Not much enamoured of hotel life, he is delighted to find that many people, like him, are always in search of the small, personal, family-run place.

In Thailand wächst die Blume *kaew*, die dem Jasmin ähnelt, häufig als Heckenpflanze. Zur Blütezeit überziehen die weißen Blüten die Hügel im Norden Chiang Mais mit einem berauschenden Duft.

Suan Kaew lautet der Name eines Dorfes vierundzwanzig Kilometer nördlich von Chiang Mai – »Garten der Kaew-Blumen«. In diesem Ort fand Vibhanand Rangsit – kurz Vip – ein Stück Land, umgeben von Reisfeldern und bewaldeten Hügeln. Er gab einem befreundeten Architekten, Archarn Dulphichai, und der Landschaftsarchitektin Patraporn Charusorn, seiner Cousine, den Auftrag, ein traditionelles Haus inmitten eines Gartens zu bauen, und war als Bauherr weise genug, sich nicht in ihre Entwürfe einzumischen. Bambushaine umgeben das Haus mit dem Steildach, das mitten in einem Garten voller verschiedener Blatt- und Blütenpflanzen steht. Mehrmals pro Woche praktiziert Vip in Bangkok als Akupunkteur. Inzwischen hat sich seine Villa mit ihrem schönen Garten (folgende Doppelseite) aber auch zu einer beliebten Pension entwickelt. Er selbst hält nicht viel von dem üblichen Hotelangebot und freut sich, dass es noch mehr Leute seiner Art gibt – die ein kleines, persönlich geführtes Gästehaus zu schätzen wissen.

On voit souvent en Thaïlande des haies de *kaew*, une fleur blanche qui ressemble au jasmin. Lorsqu'elle fleurit, Chiang Mai, ville escarpée au nord du pays, s'emplit de son parfum entêtant.

C'est dans le village de Suan Kaew (le jardin de fleurs de *kaew*), à une bonne vingtaine de kilomètres au nord de Chiang Mai, que Vibhanand Rangsit, alias Vip, a découvert un terrain parmi les rizières et les collines boisées. Il a chargé son ami, l'architecte Archarn Dulphichai, et sa cousine, l'architecte paysagiste Patraporn Charusorn, de lui construire une maison traditionnelle dans un cadre de verdure. Il a été bien inspiré de leur laisser carte blanche, car il est désormais l'heureux propriétaire d'une maison au toit très pentu qui s'élève parmi les bosquets de bambou, divers feuillages et des plantes fleuries (double page suivante). Vip, qui travaille une partie de la semaine comme acupuncteur à Bangkok, a fait de sa villa une pension ouverte sur le jardin. N'aimant guère la vie à l'hôtel, il est ravi de voir que d'autres apprécient aussi une petite maison où règne une ambiance familiale.

❊ **ABOVE AND RIGHT** a traditional woodcarving above the bed. The carpet, turtle and *thangka* are Tibetan. **FACING PAGE** The veranda floor is lined with locally-made blue tiles. **FOLLOWING PAGES** petals floating in a decorative bowl. An arrangement of flowers beside a Tibetan wallhanging with the symbol of the eternal knot. A clay image of Ganesh, the Hindu god of auspicious beginnings, is adorned with jasmine garlands. ❊ **OBEN UND RECHTS** eine traditionelle Holzschnitzarbeit über dem Bett. Der Teppich, die Schildkröte und der *Thangka* stammen aus Tibet. **RECHTE SEITE** Der Boden der Veranda wurde mit blauen Fliesen aus dem Dorf ausgelegt. **FOLGENDE DOPPELSEITEN** Blüten in einer Wasserschale. Ein Blumenarrangement neben einem tibetischen Wandbehang mit dem Symbol des unendlichen Knotens. Ganesha, die Hindu-Gottheit der verheißungsvollen Anfänge, als Tonfigur mit Jasmingirlande. ❊ **CI-DESSUS ET À DROITE** Une sculpture traditionnelle sur bois orne la tête de lit. Le tapis, la tortue et le *thangka* proviennent du Tibet. **PAGE DE DROITE** Le sol de la véranda est couvert d'un carrelage bleu fabriqué sur place. **DOUBLES PAGES SUIVANTES** un arrangement floral. Un autre arrangement floral sur l'arrière-plan d'une tenture tibétaine représentant le nœud éternel. **PAGE DE DROITE** un Ganesh hindou, la divinité des débuts prometteurs, en argile arbore un collier de jasmin. On le prie pour assurer le succès des entreprises.

Chulathat Kitibutr

Chiang Mai

A weather-beaten house in Lanna style.

Lamphun province in northern Thailand is culturally one of the oldest, most distinctive parts of the country, a melting pot of picturesque ruins, tribal style and traditional architecture.

Historically, the entire region around Chiang Mai was influenced by the traditions of the Shan-Burmese states just west of the border and of Laos to the east. Geographically juxtaposed at the crossroads, the great flowering of this culture took place during the rise of the Lanna dynasty between the 13th and 15th centuries. Lanna-style houses can be spotted a mile off, with their gabled roofs, strong teak timberwork and fretwork balconies. Chulathat Kitibutr, a distinguished professor of architecture at Chiang Mai University, is also famous for establishing the Chiang Mai Architects' Collaborative. He found this old teak house in Lamphun and reconstructed it in the village of San Pi Sear on the outskirts of Chiang Mai. The two-storeyed structure with its three linked pavilions is a restrained adaptation of a Lanna house for modern use.

Aus kultureller Sicht gilt die Provinz Lamphun in Nordthailand als eine der ältesten und bedeutendsten des Landes – mit ihrer aufregenden Mischung aus malerischen Ruinen, alten Stammesbauten und traditioneller Architektur.

Historisch gesehen stand die gesamte Region um Chiang Mai unter dem Einfluss der Shan-birmanischen Länder im Westen sowie aus Laos im Osten. Die Blütezeit dieser Kultur war hier, am geografischen Schnittpunkt der beiden Einflüsse, an den Aufstieg der Lanna-Dynastie vom 13. bis zum 15. Jahrhundert gekoppelt. Häuser im Lanna-Stil sind von weitem an ihren Giebeldächern, dem mächtigen Holzgebälk aus Teak und den durchbrochenen Balkonen zu erkennen. Chulathat Kitibutr lehrt als Architekturprofessor an der Universität von Chiang Mai und gründete ebendort auch eine Architektengemeinschaft. Der weithin anerkannte Gelehrte fand sein Haus in der Provinz Lamphun und ließ es in San Pi Sear, einem Dorf am Stadtrand von Chiang Mai, wieder aufbauen. Das zweistöckige Gebäude mit den drei Pavillons verbindet die zurückhaltende Version eines Lanna-Hauses mit den modernen Bedürfnissen seiner Bewohner.

Sur le plan culturel, la province de Lamphun, dans le nord de la Thaïlande, est l'une des régions les plus anciennes et les plus caractéristiques du pays. Elle marie des ruines pittoresques, le style tribal et l'architecture traditionnelle.

Au fil des siècles, la région de Chiang Mai a subi l'influence des Etats shan birmans à l'ouest, et du Laos à l'est. Carrefour de civilisations, cette région a été florissante pendant l'âge d'or du royaume de Lan Na, entre les 13e et 15e siècles. Les maisons de style Lan Na, avec leurs toits à pignons, leur solide charpente de teck et leurs balcons aux rambardes richement ouvragées se remarquent à une lieue à la ronde. C'est Chulathat Kitibutr, éminent professeur d'architecture à l'université de Chiang Mai et fondateur de l'association regroupant les architectes de cette ville, qui a déniché cette vieille maison de teck à Lamphun et l'a reconstruite dans le village de San Pi Sear, à la périphérie de Chiang Mai. Cette construction sur deux niveaux, à laquelle sont reliés trois pavillons, correspond à une typologie traditionnelle légèrement adaptée pour un usage moderne.

※ **BELOW AND FACING PAGE** a comfortable daybed on the wooden deck that surrounds the swimming pool. At the back, a wooden walkway links the upper storey of the main house to a Lanna-style pavilion. ※ **UNTEN UND RECHTE SEITE** ein bequemes Ruhebett auf der Holzterrasse am Swimmingpool. Im Hintergrund verbindet ein Laufgang aus Holz das Obergeschoss des Haupthauses mit einem Pavillon im Lanna-Stil. ※ **CI-DESSOUS ET PAGE DE DROITE** Un confortable lit de repos sur la terrasse de la piscine. A l'arrière-plan, une passerelle en bois relie l'étage supérieur du bâtiment principal à l'un des pavillons de style Lan Na.

※ **PREVIOUS PAGES** The main staircase to the house joins the wooden walkway above. The terra cotta images were crafted by local potters. The caned reclining chair and stool were made in Chiang Mai. **ABOVE** A Lanna-style image of the Buddha stands in a niche. **FACING PAGE** The black bathtub with a wooden surround gives onto a balcony overlooking the swimming pool.
※ **VORHERGEHENDE DOPPELSEITE** Die Haupttreppe zum Haus stößt auf den erhöhten hölzernen Gang. Die Terrakottafiguren wurden von einheimischen Töpfern hergestellt. Liegestuhl und Hocker wurden in Chiang Mai von Rohrflechtern gefertigt. **OBEN** Eine Buddhafigur im Lanna-Stil wird in einer Nische ausgestellt. **RECHTE SEITE** Um die schwarze Badewanne herum wurde Holzboden verlegt. An das Bad grenzt ein Balkon mit Blick auf den Swimmingpool. ※ **DOUBLE PAGE PRECEDENTE** Le grand escalier débouche sur la passerelle de bois à l'étage. Les statues en terre cuite sont l'œuvre de potiers locaux. Le fauteuil et le repose-pied cannés ont été fabriqués à Chiang Mai. **CI-DESSUS** dans une niche, un bouddha dans le style de Lan Na. **PAGE DE DROITE** La baignoire noire est sertie dans un habillage de bois. Du balcon adjacent, on a vue sur la piscine.

Swairiang Guesthouse
Chiang Mai

A contemplative hideaway.

The moated city of Chiang Mai grew on the banks of the River Mae Nam Ping as a prosperous trading post on the medieval caravan route between China's Yunnan province and the ports of Myanmar.

Further south along the riverbank, a short drive from the city centre, are older excavated ruins at Wiang Kum Kam that date from an earlier kingdom established by Burmese Mon kings in the eleventh century. The landscape is an amateur archaeologist's delight – remains of Mon-style temples and old stones and bricks from crumbling stupas litter the landscape. One of the attractions of Wiang Kum Kam is the pleasant waterside Swairiang Guesthouse, its cottages and rooms set around a lotus-filled pond. Swairiang is composed of old Lanna-style houses and pavilions with thatched roofs restored by a Bangkok-based architect. Wiang Kum Kam is an idyllic village getaway from bustling, tourist-filled Chiang Mai. One quick way of getting there is by bicycle or on one of the motorized local three-wheelers known as *tuk-tuk*.

Die von einem Wassergraben umgebene Stadt Chiang Mai entwickelte sich am Ufer des Mae Nam Ping aus einem aufstrebenden Handelsplatz auf der mittelalterlichen Karawanenroute, die die chinesische Provinz Yunnan mit den birmanischen Häfen verband.

Nur eine kurze Autofahrt vom Zentrum entfernt liegen weiter südlich am Ufer die ausgegrabenen Ruinen von Wiang Kum Kam. Sie stammen aus dem 11. Jahrhundert, der Zeit des Königreichs der birmanischen Mon-Dynastie. Amateurarchäologen kommen in dieser Landschaft auf ihre Kosten, denn sie ist reich an Tempeln im Mon-Stil sowie alten Steinen und Ziegeln bröckelnder Stupas. In Wiang Kum Kam befindet sich direkt am Wasser das angenehme Swairiang Guesthouse, dessen Häuschen und Zimmer um einen Teich mit Lotusblüten gruppiert sind. Swairiang besteht aus alten Häusern im Lanna-Stil sowie strohgedeckten Pavillons, die von einem in Bangkok ansässigen Architekten restauriert wurden. Ein Kurztrip mit dem Fahrrad oder einem der motorisierten Dreiräder namens *tuk-tuk*, und im Nu erreicht man das idyllische Dorf Wiang Kum Kam und kann sich von dem geschäftigen Treiben in Chiang Mai erholen.

Située sur les rives de la Mae Nam Ping, Chiang Mai était un comptoir florissant sur la route que les caravanes empruntaient au Moyen Age entre la province chinoise du Yunnan et les ports birmans.

A quelques kilomètres du centre ville, plus au sud, on a mis au jour sur le site de Wiang Kum Kam les ruines d'un royaume plus ancien fondé par les rois Môn de Birmanie au 11e siècle. L'archéologue amateur y est comblé : des vestiges de temples dans le style Môn et des pierres et briques provenant de stupas en ruine émaillent le paysage. L'une des attractions de Wiang Kum Kam est la pension Swairiang, un ensemble de bungalows et de villas disposés autour d'un étang recouvert de lotus. L'architecture de Swairiang, avec ses toits en chaume restaurés par un architecte de Bangkok, est typique du style de Lan Na. Wiang Kum Kam est un village idyllique où l'on peut fuir la très touristique et trépidante Chiang Mai. Le moyen de transport le plus rapide pour s'y rendre est la bicyclette ou le *tuk-tuk*, un tricycle motorisé.

※ **PREVIOUS PAGES** The entrance hall of Swairiang the Guesthouse is decorated with local artifacts from the Chiang Mai region. **FACING PAGE** Swairiang's special suites are raised above the lotus ponc on strong wooden beams. An antique lamp hangs from a hexagonal glass-paned skylight inspired by the roofs of Buddhist temples. **ABOVE** The restaurant extends to a wooden terrace by the lotus pool for outdoor dining. ※ **VORHERGEHENDE DOPPELSEITE** Die Eingangshalle des »Swairiang Guesthouse« ist mit einheimischen Objekten aus der Gegend von Chiang Mai dekoriert. **LINKE SEITE** Mächtige Holzpfeiler stützen die Suiten über dem Lotusteich. Eine antike Lampe schwingt von einem sechseckigen Oberlicht aus Milchglas. Das Dach wurde den Dächern buddhistischer Tempel nachempfunden. **OBEN** Auf der Holzterrasse des Restaurants am Lotusteich kann man unter freiem Himmel speisen. ※ **DOUBLE PAGE PRECEDENTE** Des objets fabriqués dans la région de Chiang Mai sont exposés dans le hall d'entrée. **PAGE DE GAUCHE** Reposant sur de robustes pilotis, les suites spéciales de la pension semblent flotter au-dessus des lotus. Une lampe ancienne descend de la lucarne vitrée hexagonale, emprunt aux toits des temples bouddhiques. **CI-DESSUS** Sur la terrasse en caillebotis du restaurant, on peut prendre scn repas en contemplant le bassin aux lotus.

A Rice Barge Ayuthaya

Among the stupas in a barge of old Siam.

For about four hundred years the city of Ayuthaya, north of Bangkok, was the royal capital of Siam.

Three rivers and a canal cradle the city in a holy circle; images of Buddha, cast in bronze and stone, are consecrated among the scattering of temples and shimmering, painted stupas in the surrounding countryside. Long-tailed barges once carried cargoes of rice harvest downstream to Bangkok; now they ferry visitors to the temples or on leisurely trips to view scenes of river life. "The Golden Naga" is one such barge that Jean-Michel Beurdeley, a longtime resident of Thailand, bought in 1999 and restored as a houseboat powered by a diesel engine. The hold was converted into a master bedroom and two smaller rooms added to create an elegant suite. Passengers can move around the galley for fresh air or lounge on the roof in the evenings. The barge, built from a superb golden teak, gleams with renewed health after its facelift.

Vierhundert Jahre lang war Ayutthaya im Norden von Bangkok Hauptstadt des Königreiches Siam.

Drei Flüsse und ein Kanal fließen in einem heiligen Kreis um die Stadt herum. In den Tempeln der Stadt stehen zahlreiche Buddhastatuen aus Bronze oder Stein. Auf dem Land dagegen finden sich glänzend bemalte Stupas. Die langen Reisbarken, mit denen einst die Reisernte flussabwärts nach Bangkok transportiert wurde, dienen inzwischen als Fähren zu den Tempeln oder als Ausflugsboote, von denen aus man das Leben am Fluss bestaunen kann. Jean-Michel Beurdeley lebt seit langem in Thailand und kaufte 1999 eine solche Barke namens »The Golden Naga«. Er baute sie zu einem dieselbetriebenen Hausboot um. Der Lagerraum wurde in ein großes Schlafzimmer verwandelt, das mit den beiden kleineren Räumen eine elegante Suite bildet. Die Passagiere können sich auf der Barke aus feinem goldschimmerndem Teakholz frei bewegen, frische Luft schnappen oder die Abende auf dem Dach verbringen.

Ayutthaya, au nord de Bangkok, a été la capitale du royaume de Siam pendant quatre siècles.

Trois rivières et un canal forment un cercle sacré autour de la ville. On peut admirer des statues de Bouddha, en bronze ou en pierre, dans les temples, et des stupas peints aux couleurs chatoyantes dans la campagne environnante. De longues barges acheminaient autrefois du riz vers Bangkok, en aval; maintenant, elles amènent les visiteurs aux temples ou les emmènent en excursion. En 1999, Jean-Michel Beurdeley, qui réside depuis longtemps en Thaïlande, a fait l'acquisition d'une barge de ce type, et l'a transformée en house-boat équipé d'un moteur diesel. La cale de « The Golden Naga » a été convertie en une suite élégante, composée d'une chambre principale et de deux chambres plus petites. Les passagers peuvent se promener sur l'embarcation pour prendre l'air ou passer leur soirée sur le pont. Une fois restaurée, cette barge, construite dans un superbe teck blond, a retrouvé toute sa splendeur passée.

PREVIOUS PAGES captain and caretaker of the "Golden Naga" in attendance. the dining and lounge areas. Cabin bathrooms with showers. **ABOVE** The reclining Buddha at the Wat Yai Chai Mongkol in Ayuthaya. **FACING PAGE** The Wat's tall chedi is Ayuthaya's landmark. Smaller chedis on a square platform face the major one. Buddha idols, decked for the rainy season, surround the temple complex. ❊ **VORHERGEHENDE DOPPELSEITE** im Dienst – der Kapitän und der Verwalter der »Golden Naga«. Der Speisesaal und die Lounge. Die Badezimmer in der Kabine verfügen über Duschen. **OBEN** der berühmte Liegende Buddha des Wat Yai Chai Mongkol in Aythaya. **RECHTE SEITE** Der riesige Chedi des Wats ist das Wahrzeichen von Ayuthaya. Von einem erhöhten viereckigen Podium aus sind kleinere Chedis dem Großen zugewandt. Rund um die Tempelanlage stehen Buddhafiguren, die für die Regenzeit hergerichtet wurden. ❊ **DOUBLE PAGE PRECEDENTE** le capitaine et le gardien du « Golden Naga » en service. Espace salon-salle à manger. cabines avec douche. **CI-DESSUS** le Bouddha allongé du Vat Yai Chai Mongkol, à Ayuthaya. **PAGE DE DROITE** Le chedi élevé du vat est l'emblème d'Ayuthaya. Sur un socle carré, des chedis de dimensions plus modestes font face au chedi central. Des représentations du Bouddha, recouvertes ici pour la saison des pluies, émaillent le complexe religieux.

Rolf and Helen von Bueren

Bangkok

A rambling tropical estate.

With their mixed Thai and European ancestry, and their reputation as collectors and designers of fine handcrafted jewellery and objets d'art in long-established "Lotus Arts de Vivre" outlets in Asia, Rolf and Helen von Bueren, together with their two handsome sons Sri and Nicklas, represent the best of international taste and Asian family values.

Their remarkable work – a jade mouse with ruby eyes or a tortoiseshell box with filigreed gold clasp – is produced as a series of individual treasures; it is only matched by the enchantment of their homes in Bangkok and Bali or their life-enhancing hospitality and exuberant high spirits. German-born Rolf came to Thailand more than four decades ago but it was his Thai wife Helen who originated the family business. In the heart of Bangkok, four generations of the family live in a series of traditional Thai houses arranged in a garden estate – a tribute to continuity and the changing fashions of cosmopolitan style.

Rolf und Helen von Bueren repräsentieren, zusammen mit ihren gut aussehenden Söhnen Sri und Nicklas, aufgrund ihrer thailändischen und europäischen Wurzeln und ihrem Ruf als Sammler und Designer eine ausgezeichnete Mischung aus international geprägtem Geschmack und asiatischen Familienwerten. Unter dem Markennamen »Lotus Arts de Vivre« entwerfen sie in Handarbeit hergestellte Schmuckstücke und Kunstgegenstände.

Ihre bemerkenswerten Arbeiten – beispielsweise eine Maus aus Jade mit Augen aus Rubinen oder ein Kästchen aus Schildpatt mit filigranem Goldverschluss – werden sorgfältig zu einzigartigen Wertgegenständen gefertigt und höchstens noch übertroffen von der Atmosphäre in ihren Häusern in Bangkok und Bali. Im Einklang mit ihren Kreationen stehen ihre großzügige Gastfreundschaft und ihre mitreißend gute Laune. Der deutschstämmige Rolf kam bereits vor mehr als vierzig Jahren nach Thailand, aber es war seine Frau Helen, die das Familiengeschäft ins Leben rief. Vier Generationen dieser Familie leben in einer Gartenanlage mitten in Bangkok in mehreren traditionellen thailändischen Häusern – ein Tribut an Beständigkeit und Wechsel kosmopolitischen Stils.

Avec leur double ascendance européenne et thaïe et leur solide réputation de collectionneurs et de créateurs de bijoux et d'objets d'art pour la chaîne Lotus Arts de Vivre solidement établie en Asie, Rolf et Helen von Bueren, et leurs fils Sri et Nicklas, représentent le meilleur du goût international et des valeurs familiales asiatiques.

Leurs créations remarquables, par exemple une souris en jade aux yeux de rubis ou une boîte en écaille de tortue dotée d'un fermoir en or ouvragé, sont des trésors uniques qui n'ont d'égal que le charme de leurs résidences à Bangkok et Bali ou leur hospitalité chaleureuse et leur formidable entrain. Né en Allemagne, Rolf est arrivé en Thaïlande il y a une bonne quarantaine d'années. Son épouse Helen, thaïlandaise, est à l'origine de l'entreprise familiale. Quatre générations de la famille vivent au cœur de Bangkok, dans des maisons thaïes traditionnelles disséminées dans une propriété paysagère, – un hommage à la continuité et aux modes cosmopolites changeantes.

❊ **ABOVE** Stairs lead to a traditional house elevated on pillars. **RIGHT** Tibetan rugs and antique images in the bathroom. **FACING PAGE** Burmese lacquer bowls on a gilt Thai cabinet in a dining room corner. **FOLLOWING PAGES** A former rice barn is converted into the dining room with low seating. A Burmese musical instrument in the form of a *naga* dominates the setting. ❊ **OBEN** Eine Treppe führt zu einem traditionellen Haus auf Säulen. **RECHTS** Tibetische Teppiche und antike Statuen im Badezimmer. **RECHTE SEITE** Birmanische Lackschüsseln auf einem vergoldeten thailändischen Schrank in einer Ecke des Speisezimmers. **FOLGENDE DOPPELSEITE** Eine ehemalige Reisscheune wurde in ein Speisezimmer mit niedrigen Sitzgelegenheiten verwandelt. Im Zentrum steht ein birmanisches Musikinstrument in Form einer *naga*. ❊ **CI-DESSUS** Un escalier mène à cette maison traditionnelle sur pilotis. **A DROITE** Des tapis tibétains et des antiquités agrémentent la salle de bains. **PAGE DE DROITE** Dans un coin de la salle à manger, des récipients en laque birmans sont exposés sur un meuble doré thaï. **DOUBLE PAGE SUIVANTE** Cette salle à manger où l'on prend ses repas assis sur des coussins est un ancien grenier à riz. Un instrument de musique en forme de *naga* constitue la pièce maîtresse de la décoration.

Jean-Michel and Patsri Beurdeley
Bangkok

Asian art in a luxuriant courtyard setting.

In the early 1970s, Jean-Michel Beurdeley's wife Patsri received an unexpected gift from her mother: a plot near Ramkhamhaeng University. Like a great deal of land in Bangkok, the property was a swamp.

The Beurdeleys decided to build a traditional house on stilts to prevent damage from flooding, going in for the strong, big-roofed style characteristic of architecture in northern Thailand. A fourth-generation art collector, the Paris-born Beurdeley has a weakness for homes that open into courtyards and gardens. The couple was also influenced by Japanese sliding doors with their easy access to the outdoors. Eventually the house grew in four separate sections around a central courtyard and swimming pool with shady terraces. For many years Beurdeley ran a successful gallery of Asian art in Paris. It was inevitable that one section would become a gallery. The box-like structure, also on stilts, has a roof made of cables, not tiles. Creepers form a natural ceiling to displays of modern art by Thai artists.

Anfang der 1970er Jahre erhielt Jean-Michel Beurdeleys Frau Patsri ein unerwartetes Geschenk von ihrer Mutter: ein Grundstück in der Nähe der Ramkhamhaeng-Universität. Allerdings bestand es, wie viele andere in Bangkok, zunächst vor allem aus Sumpfland.

Die Beurdeleys beschlossen, dort einen in Nordthailand üblichen Pfahlbau in Form eines mächtigen Gebäudes mit einem großen Dach zu bauen. Beurdeley, der ursprünglich aus Paris stammende Kunstsammler in vierter Generation, hat eine Vorliebe für Häuser mit Innenhöfen und Gärten. Außerdem bevorzugt das Paar japanische Schiebetüren, die den Übergang zwischen Drinnen und Draußen ineinander gleiten lassen. Schließlich wurde das Haus in vier verschiedenen Teilen rund um einen Innenhof mit Swimmingpool und schattigen Terrassen gebaut. Da Beurdeley in Paris lange Jahre erfolgreich eine Galerie mit asiatischer Kunst leitete, wurde in einem Teil des Hauses ebenfalls eine Galerie eingerichtet. Der Kastenbau steht ebenfalls auf Pfählen und hat ein Dach aus Kabeln statt aus Ziegeln. Kletterpflanzen bilden, passend zu den ausgestellten modernen Kunstwerken thailändischer Künstler, eine natürliche Decke.

Au début des années 1970, Patsri, la femme de Jean-Michel Beurdeley, a eu la surprise de se voir offrir par sa mère un terrain situé près de l'université de Ramkhamhaeng. Comme c'est généralement le cas à Bangkok, il était situé dans une zone marécageuse.

Les Beurdeley ont choisi une construction sur pilotis – pour éviter les risques d'inondation –, qui présente le toit massif traditionnel, caractéristique du nord de la Thaïlande. Collectionneur d'art de quatrième génération, ce Parisien aime les maisons donnant sur des cours et des jardins et partage avec son épouse le goût pour les portes coulissantes japonaises, qui permettent d'accéder facilement à l'extérieur. Ainsi leur demeure est composée de quatre bâtiments disposés autour d'une cour centrale et d'une piscine ombragée. Jean-Michel Beurdeley ayant dirigé avec succès pendant de nombreuses années une galerie d'art asiatique à Paris, il allait de soi qu'un des bâtiments deviendrait une galerie. Cette construction en forme de boîte reposant sur des pilotis est surmontée d'un toit en câbles, et non en tuiles. Les plantes grimpantes mettent en valeur des œuvres d'art moderne réalisées par des artistes thaïs.

FACING PAGE The 19th-century wood carving of the monkey god is from northern Thailand. Orchids in glazed urns line a terrace by the swimming pool. **ABOVE** The seating area by the swimming pool is covered with trailing vines. **FOLLOWING PAGES** an 18th-century image of a Chinese deity. A painting by Thai artist Tawan Dachanee covers an entire wall of the living room. a stone Buddha's torso on a Thai cabinet, temple shutters from northern Thailand and a Burmese copper chandelier in the guest room. ❊ **LINKE SEITE** Die holzgeschnitzte Darstellung des Affengottes stammt aus Nordthailand. Orchideen in glasierten Töpfen schmücken die Terrasse am Swimmingpool. **OBEN** Reben geben in der Sitzecke am Swimmingpool Schatten. **FOLGENDE DOPPELSEITE** Das Standbild einer chinesischen Gottheit stammt aus dem 18. Jahrhundert. Das Gemälde des thailändischen Künstlers Tawan Dachanee nimmt im Speisezimmer eine ganze Wand ein. Der steinerne Torso einer Buddhafigur auf einem thailändischen Schrank. Fensterläden aus Tempeln in Nordthailand und ein birmanischer Kerzenleuchter aus Kupfer im Gästezimmer. ❊ **PAGE DE GAUCHE** Ce dieu-singe sculpté sur bois provient du nord du pays. Des orchidées dans des pots vernissés bordent la piscine. **CI-DESSUS** un coin repos sous la treille près de la piscine. **DOUBLE PAGE SUIVANTE** Cette statue de divinité chinoise date du 18e siècle. Un tableau de l'artiste thaï Tawan Dachanee couvre un mur du salon. Dans la chambre d'amis, un torse en pierre du Bouddha sur un meuble thaï, des volets provenant d'un temple du nord de la Thaïlande et un chandelier en cuivre birman.

Sri's Garden House Bangkok

On the edge of a lotus-filled lake.

Stepping from the heat and dust of Bangkok into the private preserve of the Von Bueren family in the heart of the city, visitors are often stunned. It is like entering a magic garden, with trees and trailing vines draping old Khmer and Ming statuary.

Hidden here and there are traditional houses and pavilions, and the whole exquisitely ordered jungle overlooks a lotus-filled lake with an old rice barge, converted into a small guest house. Sri von Bueren, elder son of Rolf and Helen von Bueren, lives with his wife Rai and their two small boys in a house called *Suan Sai Tan* which is Thai for "garden". Although the Von Bueren family occupies separate houses in different parts of the compound, the parent house remains the centre of activity. "It's the traditional way of living in Asia," says Bangkok-born Sri, who handles the creative side of the family business. "My mother is a great cook so all the boys hang out in the kitchen. We are so lucky – to live, work, travel and have fun together."

Besucher staunen, wenn sie, mitten aus der Hitze und dem Staub Bangkoks, in die Privatdomäne der Familie von Bueren eintauchen – als beträten sie einen Zaubergarten, in dem sie unter Bäumen und Ranken manch alte Statue aus der Zeit der Khmer und Ming finden.

Hier und da finden sich überdies traditionelle Häuser und Pavillons, und zu allem Überfluss gruppiert sich dieser wohl organisierte Dschungel um einen See mit Lotusblüten, in dem eine alte Reisbarke in ein kleines Gästehaus umgebaut wurde. Sri von Bueren, der ältere Sohn von Rolf und Helen von Bueren, wohnt mit seiner Frau Rai und ihren beiden kleinen Jungen in einem Haus namens *Suan Sai Tan*, was auf Thai »Garten« bedeutet. Obwohl die von Buerens mehrere Häuser in verschiedenen Winkeln des Anwesens bewohnen, findet das wahre Leben noch immer im Elternhaus statt. »Das entspricht der traditionellen asiatischen Lebensart«, erklärt Sri, der in Bangkok geboren wurde und den kreativen Bereich des Familiengeschäfts leitet. »Meine Mutter ist eine großartige Köchin, deshalb treffen sich alle Jungs immer in der Küche. Wir haben das unglaubliche Glück, dass wir zusammen leben, arbeiten, reisen und Spaß haben können.«

Les visiteurs qui arrivent de la touffeur et poussière de Bangkok dans le petit paradis de la famille von Bueren au cœur de la ville, sont souvent ébahis. C'est comme s'ils entraient dans un jardin enchanté abritant des statues anciennes Khmer et Ming sous les arbres et les treilles.

Dissimulés ça et là dans cette jungle admirablement ordonnée, des pavillons et maisons traditionnelles sont groupés autour d'un lac où fleurissent les lotus, sur lequel une barge pour le transport du riz a été convertie en petit appartement pour les invités. Sri von Bueren, l'aîné de Rolf et Helen von Bueren, vit avec son épouse Rai et ses deux jeunes fils dans une maison appelée *Suan Sai Tan*, «jardin» en thaï. Bien que chaque membre de la famille ait son foyer dans un endroit retiré de la propriété, la maison des parents reste le point de convergence. «C'est le mode de vie traditionnel en Asie», explique Sri, né à Bangkok, le créatif de l'entreprise familiale. «Ma mère est si bonne cuisinière que tous les garçons sont toujours pendus à ses basques. Nous avons beaucoup de plaisir à vivre, travailler et voyager ensemble.»

※ **ABOVE** The dining area on the lotus-filled lake is a wooden pavilion screened with bamboo blinds. **BELOW LEFT** A low carved bed in the bedroom also overlooks the lake. **BELOW RIGHT** Another view of the pavilion. ※ **OBEN** In einem Holzpavillon mit Bambusrollos über dem Lotussee liegt der Essbereich. **UNTEN LINKS** ein niedriges holzgeschnitztes Bett im Schlafzimmer, das ebenfalls auf den See hinausgeht. **UNTEN RECHTS** eine weitere Außenansicht des Pavillons. ※ **CI-DESSUS** La salle à manger au-dessus du lac a été aménagée dans un pavillon en bois protégé par des stores en bambou. **CI-DESSOUS, À GAUCHE** Du lit bas en bois sculpté, on peut aussi contempler le lac. **CI-DESSOUS, À DROITE** le pavillon vu sous un autre angle.

※ **ABOVE** A dramatic cabinet from northern Thailand stands at the far end of the living room. **BELOW LEFT** The living room underneath the main house overlooks the lake. The carved table is Chinese. **BELOW RIGHT** The walls and floor of the interiors are of teak panels. **FOLLOWING PAGES** detail of heliconia blossoms in the garden. ※ **OBEN** Ein reich verzierter Schrank aus Nordthailand steht ganz hinten im Wohnzimmer. **UNTEN LINKS** Ausblick von dem Wohnzimmer unter dem Haupthaus auf den See. Der holzgeschnitzte Tisch stammt aus China. **UNTEN RECHTS** Innen sind Wände und Böden mit Teakholz verkleidet. **FOLGENDE DOPPELSEITE** Detailansicht der Helikonienblüten im Garten. ※ **CI-DESSUS** Un meuble spectaculaire provenant du nord de la Thaïlande occupe le fond du salon. **CI-DESSOUS, À DROITE** Le salon sous la maison principale donne sur le lac. La table en bois sculptée est originaire de Chine. **CI-DESSOUS, À GAUCHE** Les murs et les parquets sont en teck. **DOUBLE PAGE SUIVANTE** gros plan sur des fleurs de balisier dans le jardin.

The Maha Bhetra Phuket

A yacht goes with the flow.

Paris-based American architect Ed Tuttle has moved between Europe and Asia for 30 years, and is distinguished for his design of several hotels and resorts.

Asked to design a yacht for a private client to be moored on the west coast of Thailand, he couldn't see the point of a high-tech cruiser; Tuttle is a firm believer in combining indigenous skills with a harmony of materials. In creating the *Maha Bhetra*, which means "Boat" in Thai, he literally went with the flow. The 90-foot wooden motor boat was crafted by traditional boat-builders in Phuket from local varieties of teak. It has three identical main cabins with woven cane panels set in teak frames; the upper deck has a covered seating and dining area that opens on to a sun deck. Tuttle's interiors are a stylishly simple tribute to quality materials and local antiques. The Maha Bhetra sails among the many jewel-like uninhabited islands near the border to Myanmar and the Malaysian peninsula.

Der in Paris ansässige amerikanische Architekt Ed Tuttle reiste 30 Jahre lang zwischen Europa und Asien. Verschiedene Ferienanlagen und Hotels tragen die Handschrift des hoch gelobten Designers.

Als er darum gebeten wurde, eine Yacht zu entwerfen, die an der Westküste Thailands ankern sollte, lehnte Ed Tuttle es ab, einen weiteren Hightech-Cruiser zu bauen. Da er stets die Geschicklichkeit der Einheimischen mit harmonischem Baumaterial in Verbindung bringen möchte, schwamm er beim Entwurf der *Maha Bhetra*, was auf Thai »Boot« bedeutet, buchstäblich mit dem Strom. Traditionell ausgebildete Bootsbauer zimmerten die neunzig Meter lange Yacht in Phuket aus verschiedenen Teakhölzern. Das Schiff hat drei identische Kabinen mit geflochtenen, in Rahmen aus Teakholz gefassten Rohrplatten. An Deck wurde ein Bereich überdacht, der zum Sitzen und Speisen einlädt. Daran schließt sich ein Sonnendeck an, und auch die Innenräume wurden von Tuttle schlicht, aber mit allem Komfort, aus wertvollem Baumaterial und mit Antiquitäten aus der Umgebung eingerichtet. Die Maha Bhetra segelt zwischen den vielen kleinen Inseln unweit der birmanischen Grenze und der malaysischen Halbinsel.

Ed Tuttle, architecte américain établi à Paris et connu pour ses nombreux hôtels et stations balnéaires, a passé 30 ans de sa vie entre l'Europe et l'Asie.

Un jour, un particulier lui a commandé les plans d'un yacht censé avoir son port d'attache sur la côte ouest de la Thaïlande. Fervent adepte du savoir-faire local et d'une harmonie des matériaux, Ed Tuttle a écarté l'idée d'un bateau de croisière high-tech. Et en concevant le *Maha Bhetra* – «Bateau» en thaï –, il n'a fait que suivre ses penchants. C'est ainsi que cette embarcation à moteur de 30 mètres de long a été fabriquée dans des essences locales de teck par des artisans de Phuket. Les trois cabines principales du Maha Bhetra sont dotées de cloisons de rotin tressé montées sur des cadres en teck ; sur le pont supérieur, on trouve un espace salon et repas couvert. Les intérieurs conçus par Tuttle sont un hommage d'une grande simplicité aux matériaux de qualité et aux antiquités locales. Le Maha Bhetra vogue entre les milliers d'îlots inhabités qui émaillent la mer aux abords de la frontière birmane et de la péninsule malaisienne.

※ **FACING PAGE** A wooden cart wheel hangs between sliding window panels. **ABOVE** banquettes covered in Jim Thompson fabric along the covered dining area on the upper deck. **BELOW** an antique spot lamp in the sunning area. ※ **LINKE SEITE** Zwischen den Schiebefenstern in der Kabine hängt ein hölzernes Wagenrad. **OBEN** Die Bänke im überdachten Speisezimmer an Deck sind mit Jim-Thompson-Stoffen gepolstert. **UNTEN** ein antiker Strahler auf dem Sonnendeck. ※ **PAGE DE GAUCHE** Une roue de charrette est accrochée entre les fenêtres coulissantes de la cabine. **CI-DESSUS** Des banquettes recouvertes de tissus signés Jim Thompson courent le long des parois de l'espace dîner sur le pont supérieur. **CI-DESSOUS** un projecteur ancien dans le solarium du pont supérieur.

A Private Holiday Villa Phuket

Sun, sand and serendipity
by the Andaman Sea.

Up until a few years ago, the land north of the tourist-filled resorts of Phuket was still wild open country. It was along this sparkling coastline – in what was once a rubber plantation – that a European couple bought into a development of villas promoted by a Thai architect.

The couple is well-known for their fine taste and, in particular, their collection of contemporary Chinese, American and Russian art. After decades of travelling in Asia, when they began to consider a permanent holiday home, Thailand was the natural choice: as much for the friendliness of its people as its political stability and easy tax regime. They had the temple-like, three-storeyed villa custom-built to their own design. A central teak and steel spiral staircase leads to the bedrooms and an office above. The floors of seasoned teak came from an old farmhouse, specially purchased for the purpose. Filled with a mixture of Asian antiques and contemporary art, it is a vacation villa that will one day, they hope, become their retirement home.

Noch bis vor wenigen Jahren herrschte nördlich der Ferienanlagen von Phuket die reine Wildnis. An dieser paradiesischen Küste kaufte sich ein europäisches Ehepaar bei einem thailändischen Architekten in ein Villenprojekt am Standort einer ehemaligen Gummiplantage ein.

Das Paar ist für seinen exquisiten Geschmack, vor allem aber wegen seiner Sammlung zeitgenössischer chinesischer, amerikanischer und russischer Kunst bekannt. Nachdem beide jahrzehntelang durch Asien gereist waren und ein festes Ferienhaus in Betracht zogen, kam als Standort nur Thailand in Frage – der freundlichen Bevölkerung, der politischen Stabilität und der laxen Steuergesetze wegen. Die tempelähnliche, dreistöckige Villa wurde nach eigenen Entwürfen gebaut: In der Mitte führt eine Wendeltreppe aus Stahl und Teak zu den Schlafzimmern und einem Arbeitszimmer. Die Böden aus abgelagertem Teakholz stammen aus einem alten Bauernhaus, das die Eigentümer eigens für diesen Zweck kauften. In der Hoffnung, eines Tages als Rentner in ihrer Villa zu wohnen, kombinierten sie liebevoll asiatische Antiquitäten mit zeitgenössischer Kunst.

Il y a encore quelques années, la région située au nord des stations balnéaires bondées de Phuket était encore sauvage. C'est sur son superbe littoral, où se trouvait autrefois une plantation d'hévéas, qu'un couple a acheté une villa dans un lotissement construit par un architecte et promoteur thaï.

Ces Européens, connus pour leur goût raffiné et, plus particulièrement pour leur collection d'art contemporain chinois, américain et russe, se sont mis en quête, après des années à voyager en Asie, d'une résidence secondaire. Leur choix s'est tout naturellement porté sur la Thaïlande, paradis fiscal à l'hospitalité légendaire et d'une grande stabilité politique. Ils ont fait construire d'après leurs propres dessins cette villa de deux étages qui ressemble à un temple. Un escalier en colimaçon en teck et acier dessert les chambres et le bureau. Les planchers en teck séché proviennent d'une vieille ferme, achetée spécialement à cet effet. Un mélange d'antiquités asiatiques et d'art contemporain agrémente cette maison de vacances qui, espèrent-ils, deviendra un jour leur domicile permanent, l'heure de la retraite venue.

❋ **FACING PAGE** The 18th-century standing Buddha in the entrance hall is Burmese. **ABOVE AND RIGHT** The Buddha theme is continued with a locally-made model in the peak-roofed bedroom and a contemporary painting acquired in Phuket. **FOLLOWING PAGES** The house opens onto a swimming pool terrace with a shingle-roofed pavilion. ❋ **LINKE SEITE** Die Buddhastatue aus dem 18. Jahrhundert in der Eingangshalle stammt aus Myanmar. **OBEN UND RECHTS** Das Buddha-Motiv wird von der einheimischen Nachbildung im Schlafzimmer unter dem Spitzdach ebenso aufgenommen wie von dem zeitgenössischen Gemälde aus Phuket. **FOLGENDE DOPPELSEITE** Das Haus verfügt über eine Terrasse mit Swimmingpool und einem Pavillon mit Schindeldach. ❋ **PAGE DE GAUCHE** Le Bouddha debout du 18e siècle dans l'entrée est originaire du Myanmar. **CI-DESSUS ET Á DROITE** Le thème du bouddha se retrouve dans une sculpture thaïe exposée dans la chambre à toit pointu et sur un tableau contemporaine acheté à Phuket. **DOUBLE PAGE SUIVANTE** La maison donne sur la terrasse de la piscine et son pavillon couvert de bardeaux.

※ **FACING PAGE** A pair of ornamental 19th-century Chinese doors lead into the dining room. All bedrooms give onto open-air shower areas. **ABOVE** In the entrance hall, a pair of 19th-century Burmese wooden figures carrying a gong stand on the long table from Shanxi province in China. **FOLLOWING PAGES** A contemporary painting by Chinese artist Li Gui Jun titled "Warm Springs" hangs in the dining room. ※ **LINKE SEITE** Reich verzierte chinesische Türen aus dem 19. Jahrhundert führen ins Speisezimmer. An jedes Schlafzimmer ist ein Badebereich mit Außendusche angeschlossen. **OBEN** Zwei birmanische Holzfiguren aus dem 19. Jahrhundert halten einen Gong in der Eingangshalle. Der Tisch stammt aus der chinesischen Provinz Shanxi. **FOLGENDE DOPPELSEITE** Im Speisezimmer hängt das zeitgenössische Gemälde des chinesischen Malers Li Gui Jun mit dem Titel »Warm Springs«. ※ **PAGE DE GAUCHE** Deux portes décoratives chinoises du 19e siècle s'ouvrent sur la salle à manger. Toutes les chambres donnent sur un espace de douche en plein air. **CI-DESSUS** Dans le hall d'entrée, deux figurines birmanes du 19e siècle en bois portant un gong sont posées sur une table en bois provenant de la province chinoise de Shanxi. **DOUBLE PAGE SUIVANTE** Dans la salle à manger, on peut admirer *Warm Springs*, un tableau moderne de l'artiste chinois Li Gui Jun.

The Three Nagas
Francis Engelmann
Madame Boupha

Laos

ROYAL PHOTO

Madame Boupha Luang Prabang

A rememberance of the past.

Even Madame Boupha, who has lived in the house since she was eight, is not quite sure how old it is. It was built by her grandfather and passed on to her through her mother.

Little has changed in this house for more than a hundred years except the front entrance which once faced the river. A relative, the abbot of a Buddhist temple, preferred a street entrance. And, yes, he also replaced the terra cotta roof tiles with cement ones, then considered modern, and put them on the front steps. He also added modern toilets but that was a long time ago. Madame Boupha was a primary school teacher but she got tired of talking to her pupils and became a housewife. She had a talent for needlework and covered clothes and curtains in gold embroidery. Her handiwork covers cushions, tablecloths and bed linen, which secured her a gradual accretion of possessions. The house has an ongoing life, like the ebb and flow of the nearby river.

Nicht einmal Madame Boupha, die seit ihrem achten Lebensjahr in diesem Haus wohnt, weiß, wie alt es ist. Ihr Großvater hat es gebaut und über ihre Mutter an sie weitervererbt.

Mehr als hundert Jahre lang wurde in dem Haus nur wenig verändert, abgesehen vom Eingang, der einst zum Fluss hin lag. Ein Verwandter, Abt eines buddhistischen Klosters, bevorzugte einen Eingang zur Straße. Außerdem ersetzte er die Dachziegel aus Terrakotta durch solche aus Zement, die damals modern waren, und ließ auch die Eingangstreppe damit auslegen. Moderne Toiletten ließ er ebenfalls einbauen, doch das ist lange her. Madame Boupha war einst Grundschullehrerin, aber eines Tages hatte sie keine Lust mehr zu unterrichten und wurde Hausfrau. Sie entdeckte ihr Handarbeitstalent und verzierte Kleidung und Vorhänge mit goldener Stickerei. Sie bestickte Kissen, Tischdecken und Bettlaken und wurde langsam wohlhabender. Das Leben im Haus ist beständig, wie Ebbe und Flut im nahe gelegenen Fluss.

Même Madame Boupha, qui habite cette maison depuis ses huit ans, n'est pas sûre de l'âge de celle-ci. Elle en a hérité de son grand-père maternel, qui l'a construite il y a un siècle.

Peu de choses ont changé ici, si n'est á l'origine l'entrée principale était face au fleuve. Un parent, supérieur d'un temple bouddhique, a un jour préféré que l'entrée donne sur la rue. Il a aussi remplacé les tuiles en terre cuite du toit par des tuiles en ciment, alors au goût du jour, et habillé le perron avec les tuiles d'origine. Il a aussi installé des toilettes modernes. Mais tout cela s'est passé il y a bien longtemps. Madame Boupha travaillait comme institutrice jusqu'au jour où elle en a eu assez d'enseigner et s'est retirée de la vie active. Très douée pour les travaux d'aiguille, elle brodait au fill d'or des vêtements et des rideaux. Elle brode aujourd'hui des coussins, des nappes, des draps et est devenue prospère. Sa maison est vivante, comme la rivière qui coule dans les parages.

※ **PREVIOUS PAGES** the entrance to Madame Boupha's house. **ABOVE** views of the living room and veranda. **BELOW AND FACING PAGE** The animal horns were gifts to her father from villagers in Phongsaly province where he was governor. ※ **VORHERGEGANGENE DOPPELSEITE** der Eingang zu Madame Bouphas Haus. **OBEN** Blick in das Wohnzimmer und auf die Veranda. **UNTEN UND RECHTE SEITE** Die Geweihe sind ein Geschenk der Dorfbewohner aus der Provinz Phongsaly, an ihren Vater, den Provinzgouverneur. ※ **DOUBLE PAGE PRECEDENTE** l'entrée de la maison de Madame Boupha. **CI-DESSUS** le salon et la véranda. **CI-DESSOUS ET PAGE DE DROITE** Les cornes d'animaux sont des présents fait à son père par des villageois de la province de Phongsaly, dont il était gouverneur.

5P
L ≤ 4.30m

The Three Nagas
Luang Prabang

A house in the city of temples.

Pascal Traham has a thing about Unesco's World Heritage cities. He studied architecture in Quebec, which is one, and eventually came to settle in Luang Prabang, which acquired World Heritage status in 1995 to preserve its unique blend of Buddhist temples and graceful French villas.

Not long ago, he took over a late 19th-century two-storeyed house that had once served as a royal lodge and later as an ice-cream factory. Close to the Nam Khan River, in the heart of Luang Prabang's historic centre, the Three Nagas, named after the guardian serpents that embellish the temples, is now an intimate hotel. Traham worked with Lao artisans using strictly traditional architectural techniques: walls were composed of bamboo treads coated with layers of lime paste; flooring and furniture were fashioned from a local wood used in boat-building. Each room gives on to wooden terraces or private verandas that offer views of temples and monks at prayer – the spiritual life of a town unchanged since medieval times.

Pascal Traham hat viel übrig für Städte, die von der Unesco zum Weltkulturerbe erklärt wurden. Er studierte in Quebec und ließ sich in Luang Prabang nieder, das diesen Status 1995 erhielt, damit die einzigartige Mischung aus buddhistischen Tempeln und anmutigen französischen Villen erhalten wird.

Vor kurzem übernahm Traham ein zweistöckiges Haus aus dem 19. Jahrhundert in der Nähe des Nam-Khan-Flusses – mitten in der Altstadt von Luang Prabang, das früher als königliche Behausung, später als Speiseeisfabrik diente. Das »Drei Nagas«, das nach den dekorativen, schützenden Schlangen in den Tempeln benannt ist, wurde inzwischen in ein gemütliches Hotel verwandelt. In Zusammenarbeit mit laotischen Handwerkern beschränkte sich Traham auf traditionelle architektonische Techniken. Die Wände bestehen aus Bambusprofilen, die schichtweise mit Kalkpaste bedeckt wurden, und sowohl die Böden als auch die Möbel wurden aus einem Holz angefertigt, das sonst im Schiffsbau verwendet wird. An jedes Zimmer schließt sich eine Holzterrasse oder eine private Veranda an, von der aus die Gäste, Tempel und Mönche beim Gebet – das spirituelle Leben einer Stadt, das sich seit dem Mittelalter kaum verändert hat – beobachten können.

Pascal Trahem est poursuivi par les villes patrimoine mondial de l'Humanité : il a fait ses études à Quebec et s'est installé à Luang Prabang. Cette ville figure sur la liste du patrimoine mondial de l'Humanité depuis 1995 afin que soit préservé son syncrétisme unique en son genre de temples bouddhiques et de ravissantes villas coloniales françaises.

Récemment, il a racheté un ancien pavillon royal de la fin du 19e siècle – une construction de deux étages qui avait par la suite hébergé une usine de crème glacée. A proximité de la Nam Kahn, au cœur du centre historique de Luang Prabang, Les Trois Nagas – ainsi nommé d'après les dieux serpents qui gardent les temples –, est maintenant un hôtel à l'ambiance familiale. Traham a travaillé avec des artisans locaux qui utilisent exclusivement des techniques de construction traditionnelles : les murs sont constitués de bandes de bambou chaulées, tandis que les sols et le mobilier ont été taillés dans un bois local utilisé en construction navale. Chaque pièce donne sur des terrasses en bois ou des vérandas privées d'où l'on peut contempler les temples et les moines en prière, témoignages de la vie spirituelle d'une ville inchangée depuis des siècles.

❊ **PREVIOUS PAGES** Monks strolling past the Three Nagas. **ABOVE** A dining corner in a suite decorated with images of celestial nymphs. ❊ **VORHERGEHENDE DOPPELSEITE** Mönche vor dem Eingang des »Drei Nagas«. **OBEN** eine Nische zum Speisen in einer Suite, die mit Intarsien von himmlischen Nymphen dekoriert ist. ❊ **DOUBLE PAGE PRECEDENTE** Les moines se promènent aux abords des Trois Nagas. **CI-DESSUS** le coin repas dans une suite décorée de nymphes célestes.

※ **ABOVE** The restored doors to a bedroom are more than a century old. The suite is decorated with silk and organza drapes and a traditional umbrella. ※ **OBEN** Die restaurierten Türen zum Schlafzimmer sind mehr als hundert Jahre alt. Die Suite ist mit Seiden- und Organzavorhängen und einem traditionellen Schirm ausgestattet. ※ **CI-DESSUS** Ces portes de chambre restaurées sont plus que centenaires. Dans la suite, drapés de soie et d'organdi et une ombrelle traditionnelle.

Francis Engelmann

Luang Prabang

How Cinderella was reincarnated by her Prince Charming.

From the veranda of Francis Engelmann's house you can see the red roof of the Vat Nong temple, one of the many Buddhist shrines that sustain the sacred life of Luang Prabang.

Engelmann is a French economist who has lived long in Laos and written books about it; he now heads the Unesco project for the conservation and development of Luang Prabang. In a personal crusade entirely fitting with his vocation, he has undertaken the restoration of one of the largest and finest of the city's colonial mansions. The house was built in 1925 by Chinese merchants who imported fine embroideries from Canton but fell on hard times when absentee landlords left it to caretakers. Engelmann has repaired the terracotta tiled roof, rebuilt the central staircase, renovated the long veranda and planted a new garden around three old mango trees. He has decorated the place with panache, using discarded objects and copying old furniture. Gone are Cinderella's dark, dreary days. She has recovered her allure and found her Prince Charming.

Von seiner Veranda aus sieht Francis Engelmann das rote Dach des Vat-Nong-Tempels, einem der vielen buddhistischen Schreine, die das heilige Leben Luang Prabangs stützen.

Der französische Wirtschaftswissenschaftler lebt schon lange in Laos und hat mehrere Bücher über das Land verfasst. Mittlerweile leitet er das Unesco-Projekt zur Bewahrung und Entwicklung von Luang Prabang. In einem privaten Kreuzzug, der sich mit seiner Berufung deckt, nahm Francis Engelmann sich der Restaurierung eines der größten und schönsten Kolonialbauwerke der Stadt an. Chinesische Händler, die feine Stickerei aus Kanton importierten, hatten es 1925 erbaut, aber in Abwesenheit der Eigentümer wurde es von den Verwaltern schwer vernachlässigt. Engelmann ließ das Dach aus Terrakottaziegeln reparieren, baute die Haupttreppe wieder auf, renovierte die lange Veranda und legte einen neuen Garten um die drei alten Mangobäume an. Außerdem dekorierte er das Haus mit großer Begeisterung mit Nachbauten alter Möbel und Objekten, die andernorts entsorgt wurden. So wurde das Haus aus seinem Aschenputteldasein zu neuem Leben erweckt.

De la véranda de Francis Engelmann, on peut voir le toit rouge du temple de Vat Nong, l'un des nombreux sanctuaires bouddhiques qui animent la vie religieuse de Luang Prabang.

Cet économiste français qui a longtemps vécu au Laos et écrit des livres sur ce pays dirige à l'heure actuelle le projet de l'Unesco pour la sauvegarde et le développement de Luang Prabang. Mû par un intérêt à la fois personnel et professionnel, il a entrepris la restauration de l'une des plus belles et plus grandes demeures coloniales de la ville. Celle-ci avait été construite en 1925 par des commerçants chinois qui importaient des broderies fines de Canton et étaient souvent en déplacement. La maison, mal entretenue, a souffert de ces absences prolongées. Engelmann a réparé le toit en tuiles de terre cuite, refait l'escalier central, rénové la longue véranda et créé un nouveau jardin autour de trois manguiers. Et il a fait preuve de beaucoup de goût pour la décoration intérieure en choisissant des objets de récupération et des copies de meubles anciens. Fini les temps sombres : Cendrillon a trouvé son Prince charmant et retrouvé sa splendeur passée.

⁜ **BELOW** A child's bed is transformed into a comfortable and colourful sofa in the living room. **FACING PAGE** A bedroom window opens into the living room. Delicately filigreed wood panels act as ventilators above the partition wall. ⁜ **UNTEN** Ein ehemaliges Kinderbett wurde in ein bequemes farbenfrohes Sofa verwandelt; es steht im Wohnzimmer. **RECHTE SEITE** Aus dem Schlafzimmerfenster blickt man ins Wohnzimmer. Die filigran geschnitzte Holztäfelung über der Trennwand dient der Ventilation. ⁜ **CI-DESSOUS** Dans le salon, un lit d'enfant a été converti en sofa confortable aux couleurs lumineuses. **PAGE DE DROITE** Par cette fenêtre intérieure, les occupants de la chambre ont vue sur le salon. Montés au-dessus des cloisons, des panneaux de bois finement sculptés assurent la circulation d'air.

Wat Sene

Luang Prabang

The chief abbot's holy abode.

Wat Sene is one of Luang Prabang's lesser-known temples, amidst a profusion of more famous places of worship that dot the historic peninsula between two rivers and the large hill of Phu Si that forms a dramatic backdrop to the town.

The monastery's full name is Wat Sene Soukharam and its importance derives from being the residence of Phra Sangkharath, the head abbot of the *sangha*, the community of monks, seen left. Like many Lao temples it was originally the gift of a king but has been restored several times, mostly recently in 1957. Wat Sene is famous for its red-painted walls, richly stencilled in gold, elaborate carved wooden decoration and fine mosaics. Built in the classic Luang Prabang temple style with curving, low-slung roofs, it is set inside an enclosed compound. A series of sublime Buddha images inside focus the mind. Small but jewel-like in its refinement and religious atmosphere, Wat Sene is Luang Prabang's little treasure.

Wat Sene, einer der weniger bekannten Tempel in Luang Prabang, liegt inmitten berühmter religiöser Stätten, die auf der historischen Halbinsel zwischen zwei Flüssen und dem großen Hügel von Phu Si – dem aufregenden Hinterland der Stadt – verstreut sind.

Die Bedeutung des Klosters – mit vollem Namen Wat Sene Soukharam – liegt darin begründet, dass Phra Sangkharath (im Bild links) – das Oberhaupt der *sangha*, der Gemeinschaft von Mönchen – hier lebt. Wie viele laotische Tempel ging auch dieser aus einem Geschenk des Königs hervor. Er wurde jedoch mehrmals restauriert – zuletzt im Jahr 1957. Heute ist Wat Sene berühmt wegen der rot gestrichenen, mit goldener Schablonenmalerei verschwenderisch verzierten Wände, der feinen Holzvertäfelung und der zarten Mosaike. Als Teil einer abgeschlossenen Tempelanlage wurde er im klassischen Tempelstil von Luang Prabang erbaut, mit gekrümmten, geneigten Dächern. Im Innern lenken zahlreiche erhabene Buddhabildnisse den Geist auf das Wesentliche. Der kleine Tempel Wat Sene erweist sich mit seiner Feinheit und seiner andächtigen Atmosphäre als Edelstein im großen Schatz von Luang Prabang.

Des nombreux temples bouddhiques de Luang Prabang, Vat Sene fait partie des lieux de culte les moins connus de cette ville située dans une péninsule historique entre deux cours d'eau et adossée à la spectaculaire colline de Phou Si.

Ce monastère, dont le nom complet est Vat Sene Soukharam, est cependant important : il s'agit de la résidence de Phra Sangkharath (page de gauche), le plus haut dignitaire de la *sangha*, la communauté des moines bouddhistes. A l'instar de nombreux temples lao, c'était à l'origine le cadeau fait par un roi à une communauté. Restauré à plusieurs reprises, la dernière fois en 1957, Vat Sene est connu pour ses murs rouges ornés de motifs à l'or réalisés au pochoir, de décorations élaborées en bois sculpté et de délicates mosaïques. Protégé par un mur d'enceinte, Vat Sene est construit dans le style de temples classique de Luang Prabang, avec des toits superposés aux arbalétriers légèrement incurvés. Il abrite une collection de bouddhas sublimes qui invitent à la méditation. Concentré de beauté et de recueillement, Vat Sene est le joyau de Luang Prabang.

※ **ABOVE** an elaborate shelter for a ritual drum used during lunar ceremonies. Guardian serpents embellish the balustrades of the entrance stairway. **FACING PAGE** The head abbot seated before his personal altar. ※ **OBEN** Unter diesem aufwändigen Baldachin wird die rituelle Trommel aufbewahrt, die bei den Mondzeremonien eingesetzt wird. Schützende Schlangen schmücken das Geländer der Eingangstreppe. **RECHTE SEITE** Das Oberhaupt der Mönche sitzt vor seinem privaten Altar. ※ **CI-DESSUS** Cette niche de toute beauté abrite un tambour utilisé à l'occasion de cérémonies lunaires. Des serpents montent la garde sur la main courante du perron. **PAGE DE DROITE** le chef de la communauté assis devant son autel personnel.

※ **ABOVE** the main image of the Buddha in the sanctum. **FACING PAGE** monks at prayer before a standing Buddha image. ※ **OBEN** das Hauptbildnis Buddhas im Allerheiligsten. **RECHTE SEITE** betende Mönche vor einer Buddha-Statue. ※ **CI-DESSUS** le plus grand bouddha du sanctuaire. **PAGE DE DROITE** Les moines prient devant une statue de Bouddha debout.

Wat Vixoun

Luang Prabang

The radiant glow of gilded Buddhas.

Wat Vixoun, also known as Wat Wisunalat, was built by King Vixoun and is the oldest temple in worship in Luang Prabang.

The original building, all in wood, burned down in 1887 when the city was attacked by "Black Banner" pirates from southern China. The present building dates from 1898, rebuilt in bricks, after the original wooden structure. Of special beauty are the sculpted doors. In 1942, a royal prince decided to transfer many antique works here and the temple became a museum. A superb collection of Buddhas in the Luang Prabang style, standing with hands by their side, are displayed in the temple. Yet another distinctive feature of the temple is the Mat Mo stupa within its precincts. *Mat Mo* means watermelon and refers to its spherical shape. King Vixoun's wife, Queen Phan Din Xieng, is said to have dedicated the original lotus-shaped stupa. The present stupa is an early 20th-century replacement. The temple is filled with the sounds of monks at prayer or going about their daily chores.

Wat Vixoun, auch unter Wat Wisunalat bekannt, wurde im 16. Jahrundert von König Vixoun errichtet. Er ist der älteste Tempel in Luang Prabang, in dem heute noch gebetet wird.

1887 brannte das ursprüngliche Holzgebäude ab, als die Stadt von »Schwarze-Fahnen«-Piraten aus Südchina angegriffen wurde. Das heutige Gebäude stammt aus dem Jahr 1898 und wurde dem Holzbau in Backstein nachempfunden. Die bildhauerisch gestalteten Türen sind besonders schön. 1942 beschloss ein königlicher Prinz, viele antike Kunstwerke in den Tempel zu schaffen. Das daraus entstandene Museum beherbergt eine einzigartige Sammlung von Buddhas im Luang-Prabang-Stil, – stehend mit den Händen an den Seiten. Darüber hinaus steht auf dem Gelände der Tempelanlage der Mat-Mo-Stupa. Mat Mo bedeutet Wassermelone und bezieht sich auf die runde Form. Angeblich war der ehemals lotusförmige Stupa der Königin Phan Din Xieng, Vixouns Ehefrau, gewidmet. Im frühen 20. Jahrhundert wurde sie durch den gegenwärtigen Stupa ersetzt. Der Tempel ist vom Klang der Gebete und den Geräuschen erfüllt, die die Mönche beim Verrichten der alltäglichen Arbeiten verursachen.

Vat Vixun, aussi connu sous le nom de Vat Visunalat, est le plus ancien temple en service de Luang Prabang. Il a été construit par le roi Vixun au 16e siècle.

Le bâtiment d'origine, construit par le roi Vixun, a été réduit en cendres en 1887, lorsque la ville fut mise à sac par les « Pavillons noirs », faction de l'armée chinoise convertie dans le banditisme. En 1898, le temple a été reconstruit en briques sur le modèle de la construction d'origine en bois. Ses portes sculptées sont d'une très grande beauté. En 1942, un prince de sang royal a décidé d'y transférer une importante collection d'antiquités. Le temple est devenu un musée, dans lequel on peut admirer une superbe collection de bouddhas dans le style de Luang Prabang, bras le long du corps. Autre centre d'intérêt dans l'enceinte même du sanctuaire, un stupa sphérique appelé *Mat Mo*, ce qui signifie pastèque. Cette construction du début du 20e siècle est venue remplacer le stupa d'origine en forme de lotus, qui aurait été une donation de l'épouse du roi Visun, la reine Phan Din Xieng. Dans tout Vat Vixun on entend les moines prier ou vaquer à leurs occupations.

※ **ABOVE** monks at study in their rooms. **BELOW AND FACING PAGE** The great Buddha image at the centre of the altar is the biggest in Luang Prabang and is surrounded by smaller antique images. **FOLLOWING PAGES** a guardian image at the entrance to the prayer chamber. ※ **OBEN** studierende Mönche in ihrem Arbeitszimmer. **UNTEN UND RECHTE SEITE** Das große Buddhabildnis in der Mitte des Altars ist das größte in Luang Prabang. Es ist von kleineren antiken Statuen umgeben. **FOLGENDE DOPPELSEITE** Die Figur am Eingang soll die Gebetshalle schützen. ※ **CI-DESSUS** les moines s'adonnant à l'étude dans leur cellule. **CI-DESSOUS ET PAGE DE DROITE** Le gigantesque bouddha figurant au centre de l'autel entouré de représentations anciennes de dimensions plus modestes est le plus grand de Luang Prabang. **DOUBLE PAGE SUIVANTE** une figure protectrice à l'entrée de la salle de prière.

Wat Xieng Thong Luang Prabang

The home of guardian serpents.

The meeting point of two rivers is a key point in sacred geography. Wat Xieng Thong, Temple of the Golden City, is located in a beautiful garden, where the smaller Nam Khan river runs into the waters of the majestic Mekong.

It is one of the most important temples in Laos and layered with legend. One has it that this was the site where two hermits who founded Luang Prabang placed a boundary stone for the new settlement. The union of the Nam Khan and Mekong is also said to be the home of two nagas, sacred serpents, who are guardians of the river. The temple as it exists today was built in 1560 by King Setthathirat, a patron of Buddhism, and remained a royal preserve until 1975. It was where Lao kings were crowned and invested with power. Near the temple's eastern gate stands a royal funeral chapel with funerary urns that commemorate members of the royal family. Like many sacred spots, it is a place where, in the words of one scholar, "Buddhist, pre-Buddhist and royal traditions met, overlapped and meshed".

In der heiligen Geografie spielt der Zusammenfluss zweier Flüsse eine große Rolle. Wat Xieng Thong, der Tempel der Goldenen Stadt, liegt in einem wunderschönen Garten, wo der schmalere Fluss Nam Khan sich in den majestätischen Mekong ergießt.

Er zählt zu den bedeutendsten Tempeln der Stadt, und es werden viele Legenden über ihn erzählt. Einer zufolge legten zwei Mönche, die Luang Prabang gegründet haben sollen, den Grenzstein für das neue Anwesen. Überdies heißt es, dass hier, wo Nam Khan und Mekong zusammenfließen, die beiden Nagas leben, heilige Schlangen und Schutzgöttinnen des Flusses. Der bis heute erhaltene Tempel wurde 1560 von König Setthathirat erbaut, einem Befürworter des Buddhismus, und blieb bis 1975 im Besitz des Königshauses. Hier wurden die laotischen Könige gekrönt, hier wurde ihnen die Macht übertragen. Unweit des Osteingangs zum Tempel steht eine königliche Begräbniskapelle mit Urnen der königlichen Familie. Wie von vielen anderen heiligen Orten sagt man auch von diesem, dass hier »budhistische, vor-buddhistische und königliche Traditionen eine ganz eigene Symbiose eingehen«.

Le confluent de deux cours d'eau est toujours un endroit important dans la géographie sacrée. Vat Xieng Thong, temple de La Ville dorée, s'élève dans un superbe jardin où la modeste Nam Khan se jette dans les eaux du majestueux Mékong.

Ce temple, un des plus importants du Laos, est auréolé de légendes. L'une d'elles rapporte que deux ermites auraient placé une borne à cet endroit, fondant ainsi la ville de Luang Prabang. Les eaux où le Mékong et la Nam Kahn se rejoignent seraient aussi la demeure de deux nagas, serpents sacrés et gardiens du fleuve. Le temple dans sa forme actuelle a été bâti en 1560 par le roi Setthathirat, un protecteur du bouddhisme, et est resté propriété royale jusqu'en 1975. C'est ici que les rois du Laos étaient couronnés et intronisés. Près de la porte est du temple, on peut voir une chapelle funéraire royale abritant des urnes à la mémoire de membres de la famille royale. Comme bien d'autres endroits disséminés dans le pays, c'est un lieu où, selon un érudit, «les traditions bouddhiques, prébouddhiques et royales se sont rencontrées, ont coexisté et ont fusionné.»

※ **ABOVE** monks at study outside the prayer room with its richly stencilled walls and columns. ※ **OBEN** studierende Mönche vor der Gebetshalle, die mit aufwändiger Schablonenbemalung auf Wänden und Säulen verziert ist. ※ **CI-DESSUS** Des moines se consacrant à l'étude à l'extérieur de la salle de prière dont les colonnes et les murs sont richement ornés de dessins au pochoir.

※ **ABOVE** monks at prayer before the gilded image of the Buddha inside the prayer room. ※ **OBEN** betende Mönche in der Gebetshalle vor dem vergoldeten Bildnis Buddhas. ※ **CI-DESSUS** Dans la salle de prière, des moines prient devant un bouddha doré.

※ **FACING PAGE** A shelter for boats, each carved from a single tree trunk, that are used in a boat festival at the end of the rainy season. A white elephant, symbol of royalty, is fashioned from a mirror work mosaic. **ABOVE** The rear wall of the prayer chamber, in classical Luang Prabang style, is embellished with a "tree of life" mosaic. **FOLLOWING PAGES** a detail of the exquisite "tree of life". ※ **LINKE SEITE** Hier liegen die Boote bis zur Feier des Bootsfestes am Ende der Regenzeit sicher. Sie wurden jeweils aus einem einzigen Baumstamm gefertigt. Als Symbol des Königtums wurde ein weißer Elefant aus Spiegelmosaik hergestellt. **OBEN** Die Rückwand der Gebetshalle wurde im klassischen Luang-Prabang-Stil mit dem Mosaik eines »Lebensbaums« verziert. **FOLGENDE DOPPELSEITE** Details des erlesenen »Lebensbaums«. ※ **PAGE DE GAUCHE** Les bateaux remisés sous cet abri ont été taillés dans des troncs d'arbre ; ils sont utilisés à l'occasion d'une fête nautique qui a lieu à la fin de la saison des pluies. Un éléphant blanc, symbole de la royauté, fait de mosaïque miroitante. **CI-DESSUS** La façade postérieure de la salle de prière, dans le style classique de Luang Prabang, est ornée d'une mosaïque représentant l'« arbre de vie ». **DOUBLE PAGE SUIVANTE** le superbe « arbre de vie ».

※ **FACING PAGE AND ABOVE** exterior view of the prayer chamber with its sloping roofs. Monks at work, repainting the stupa, enclosure walls and staircases in preparation for Lao new year celebrations. **FOLLOWING PAGES** Young monks gaze longingly at coconuts during their afternoon break. ※ **LINKE SEITE UND OBEN** Außenansicht einer Gebetshalle mit Gefälledächern. Mönche bei der Arbeit – sie streichen den Stupa an und errichten Absperrungen für die laotische Neujahrsfeier. **FOLGENDE DOPPELSEITE** In der Nachmittagspause betrachten junge Mönche sehnsüchtig die hoch hängenden Kokosnüsse. ※ **PAGE DE GAUCHE ET CI-DESSUS** la salle de prière avec ses toits caractéristiques vue de l'extérieur. Les fêtes du Nouvel An lao approchent, les moines repeignent le stupa, les murets et les escaliers. **DOUBLE PAGE SUIVANTE** Les jeunes moines regardent longuement des noix de coco pendant leur pause de l'après-midi.

Angkor's Temples

CAMBODIA

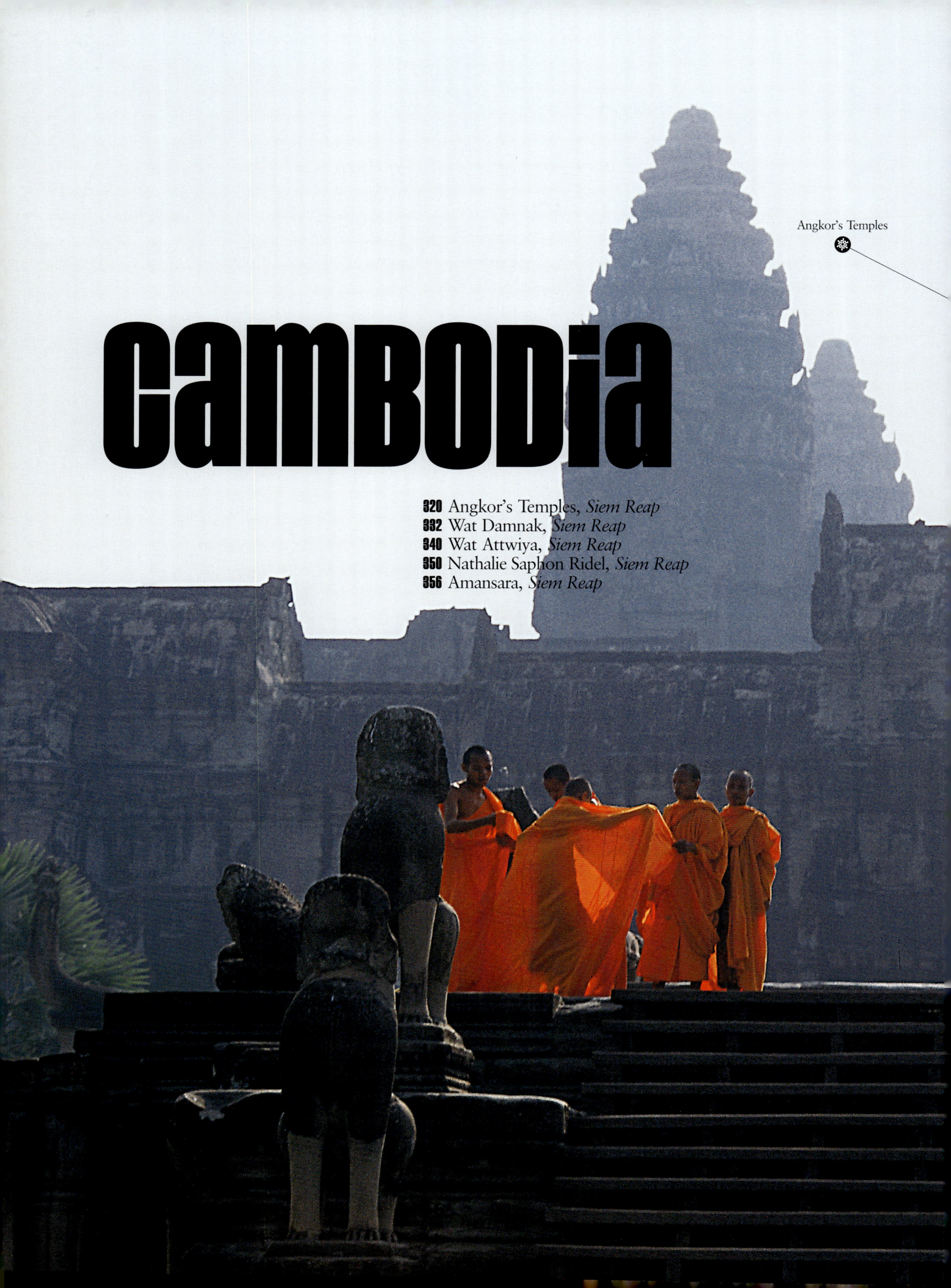

Wat Attwiya
Amansara
Wat Damnak
Nathalie Saphon Ridel

Angkor's Temples
Siem Reap

Images of gods and god-kings in a tropical jungle.

When the French naturalist Henri Mouhot came upon the magnificent ruined temples of Angkor in 1860 he asked the local people who had built them. It is the work of giants, they said.

Gigantic in scale and exquisite in sculptural detail, Angkor's temples had lain imprisoned by a tropical jungle for centuries. Mouhot's discovery created a sensation; it led to the establishment of the Ecole Française d'Extrême-Orient that since the late 19th century has tried to unlock the secrets of the powerful Khmer dynasty that built a series of royal capitals between the 9th and 13th centuries. "Unmatched in their fusion of art, architecture and philosophy," as Jon Ortner, the famous photographer of the Angkor temples put it, the citadels were built in the image of temples dedicated to Hindu gods. When the Angkor civilization declined, its temples too were abandoned, and the forest closed in. Despite decades of restoration, some monuments have been left in the embrace of nature. Roots and branches of ancient silk-cotton and strangler fig entwine the old stones, adding to Angkor's sepulchral magic.

Als der französische Naturkundler Henri Mouhot die beeindruckenden Ruinen der Tempel von Angkor 1860 entdeckte, erklärten die Einheimischen auf seine Fragen, Riesen hätten sie geschaffen.

Als Mouhots Entdeckung weltweit Aufsehen erregte, waren die riesigen Tempel von Angkor, Terrassenanlagen mit detailreicher Bauornamentik, bereits seit Jahrhunderten vom tropischen Dschungel umschlossen gewesen. Daraufhin wurde die Ecole Française d'Extrême-Orient gegründet, in deren Auftrag seit dem späten 19. Jahrhundert das Geheimnis der mächtigen Khmer-Dynastie erforscht wird, die zwischen dem 9. und 13. Jahrhundert mehrere königliche Hauptstädte erbauen ließ. Diese Zitadellen, die in »der Verschmelzung von Kunst, Architektur und Philosophie einzigartig« sind – wie Jon Ortner, der berühmte Fotograf der Angkor Tempel bemerkte –, wurden in Form von Hindu-Tempeln errichtet. Als die Angkor-Kultur unterging, wurden auch die Tempel verlassen, die in der Folgezeit vom Dschungel überwuchert wurden. Trotz der umfangreichen Restaurationsarbeiten sind einige Denkmäler noch immer der Natur überlassen. Wurzeln und Äste alter Kapokbäume und der Würgefeige umschlingen die alten Steine und tragen auf ihre Weise zu der zauberhaft düsteren Atmosphäre von Angkor bei.

Lorsqu'en 1860, le naturaliste français Henri Mouhot a découvert les impressionnantes ruines des temples d'Angkor, il a demandé aux habitants des alentours qui les avait construits. C'est l'œuvre de géants, ont-ils alors répondu.

A la fois monumentaux et d'une grande recherche dans les détails, les temples d'Angkor étaient restés prisonniers de la jungle tropicale des siècles durant. La découverte de Mouhot a fait sensation et a entraîné la création, à la fin du 19e siècle, de l'Ecole française d'Extrême-Orient. Celle-ci essaie de pénétrer les secrets de la puissante dynastie khmère qui a édifié sur ce site plusieurs capitales royales entre les 9e et 13e siècles. Ces citadelles, « sans égales dans leur fusion de l'art, de l'architecture et de la philosophie » – comme le dit Jon Ortner, le célèbre photographe des temples d'Angkor –, ont été construites sur le modèle des temples hindouistes. Avec le déclin de la civilisation d'Angkor, la forêt s'est refermée sur les temples laissés à l'abandon. Malgré un travail de restauration mené depuis des décennies, certains monuments subissent encore l'étreinte de la végétation : des racines et des branches de fromagers et de figuiers banians centenaires s'enroulent autour des vieilles pierres, ajoutant à la magie funèbre d'Angkor.

※ **PREVIOUS PAGES** a bas-relief of *apsaras*, celestial nymphs, and a statue of the Hindu god Vishnu. the entrance to the 12th-century Buddhist temple of Ta Prohm. **FACING PAGE** the south gate of the citadel of Angkor Thom. **ABOVE** 200 colossal faces of *avalokiteswaras* adorn the Bayon temple. ※ **VORHERGEHENDE DOPPELSEITEN** *Apsaras*, weibliche Geister, im Flachrelief, sowie eine Statue des Hindugottes Vishnu in Angkor Wat. Eingang zum buddhistischen Tempel Ta Prohm. **LINKE SEITE** südliches Stadttor der Zitadelle von Angkor Thom. **OBEN** 200 *avalokiteswaras*, steinerne Fratzen, schmücken den Bayon. ※ **DOUBLES PAGES PRECEDENTES** un bas-relief représentant des *apsaras*, nymphes célestes, et une statue du dieu hindouiste Vishnou. Ta Prohm, l'entrée du temple bouddhique du 12e siècle. **PAGE DE GAUCHE** la porte sud de la citadelle d'Angkor Thom. **CI-DESSUS** 200 visages géants des *avalokiteswaras* ornent le temple du Bayon.

※ **TOP** This bas-relief on the outer gallery of the Bayon temple shows cooks preparing an elaborate feast. **BOTTOM** Friezes of exquisitely jewelled *devatas*, goddesses, and celestial dancers with ornamental headdresses line the galleries of the same temple. ※ **OBEN** Flachreliefs der äußeren Galerie des Bayon zeigen Köche bei der Vorbereitung eines großen Festes. **UNTEN** Weitere Flachreliefs der Bayon-Galerien präsentieren *devatas*, Göttinnen mit erlesenem Schmuck, sowie himmlische Tänzerinnen mit verzierten Kopfbedeckungen. ※ **EN HAUT** Sur ce bas-relief visible dans la galerie extérieure du temple du Bayon, des cuisiniers s'affairent à la préparation d'un festin. **EN BAS** Les galeries du Bayon sont ornées tout du long de frises représentant des *devatas*, divinités, parées de bijoux précieux et des danseuses célestes portant des coiffes ornementales.

※ **TOP** elegantly-attired goddesses with delicately-modelled faces at the entrance to the Bayon temple. **BOTTOM** detail of a bas-relief showing a Khmer king astride an elephant leading his army into battle. ※ **OBEN** elegant gekleidete Göttinnen mit fein modellierten Gesichtern am Eingang des Bayon. **UNTEN** Detail eines Flachreliefs, auf dem der König der Khmer, auf einem Elefanten reitend, seine Armee in die Schlacht führt. ※ **EN HAUT** Des déesses aux traits délicats et parées d'élégants atours montent la garde à l'entrée du temple du Bayon. **EN BAS** Le bas-relief montre un roi khmer conduisant son armée à la bataille, monté sur un éléphant.

Wat Damnak
Siem Reap

A bridge to the Buddhist age of enlightenment.

Wat Damnak is one of the principal pagodas in Siem Reap, a temple which has undergone a remarkable resurgence in recent years to incorporate an impressive Centre for Khmer Studies.

The word *wat* does not necessarily mean only a temple; it can refer to a complex of buildings that include the main temple, a monastery and wide collection of stupas, often a school and sometimes a cremation ground. In fact a wat can be a self-contained microcosm of the Buddhist way in its purest form – of living and learning, prayer, renunciation and salvation. A wat compound may be entered from any side, but the main entrance to the temple is from the east; the central image of the Buddha always faces eastwards – as did the Buddha at the moment of his enlightenment. Wat Damnak dates from the early 20th century and was mercifully left intact by the Khmer Rouge. The plain interior of the inner sanctum, its simple colonial-style buildings and cluster of old stupas, above all its atmosphere of modern scholarship, make it a bridge between the old and new.

Wat Damnak, eine der bedeutendsten Pagoden in Siem Reap, erfährt als Tempel seit einigen Jahren zunehmendes Interesse, seit dort ein renommiertes Khmer-Forschungszentrum eingerichtet wurde.

Das Wort Wat bedeutet nicht zwangsläufig Tempel, sondern kann sich auch auf einen Gebäudekomplex mit Haupttempel, einem Kloster und zahlreichen Stupas beziehen. Häufig wurden auch noch eine Schule und ein Einäscherungsplatz angeschlossen. Tatsächlich kann ein Wat als ein in sich geschlossener Mikrokosmos des Buddhismus in Reinform betrachtet werden, wo gelebt und gelernt wird, in Gebet, Entsagung und Heil. Man kann einen Wat von allen Seiten betreten, der Haupteingang wird jedoch immer im Osten liegen, so wie auch die bedeutendste Buddha-Statue stets nach Osten blickt – wie einst Buddha im Augenblick seiner Erleuchtung. Wat Damnak wurde im frühen 20. Jahrhundert erbaut und glücklicherweise von den Roten Khmer verschont. Das karge zentrale Heiligtum mit den schlichten Gebäuden im Kolonialstil und zahlreichen alten Stupas strahlt eine Atmosphäre moderner Gelehrsamkeit aus, eine Verbindung von Alt und Neu.

Vat Damnak est l'une des principales pagodes de Siem Reap. Ce lieu de culte a connu une renaissance formidable ces dernières années et abrite désormais un impressionnant centre d'études khmères.

Le mot vat ne signifie pas uniquement temple mais peut faire référence à un complexe comprenant un temple principal, un monastère, une kyrielle de stupas et, souvent une école, plus rarement un pavillon de crémation. En fait, un vat est souvent un microcosme du bouddhisme : le mode de vie, l'étude, la prière, le renoncement et le salut y sont visibles dans la plus pure tradition. Si les ensembles bouddhiques sont ouverts à tous les vents, l'entrée principale du temple est toujours orientée à l'est et la grande statue de Bouddha regarde toujours dans cette direction, comme jadis Bouddha au moment de son Eveil. Vat Damnak, construit au début du 20e siècle, a fort heureusement été épargné par les Khmers rouges. L'intérieur sobre du sanctuaire principal, ses bâtiments de style colonial et la ribambelle de stupas anciens, et surtout son atmosphère studieuse moderne font de lui un pont entre l'ancien et le moderne.

Wat Attwiya
Siem Reap

Buddha's Middle Path.

Wat Attwiya is beautifully situated at the end of a winding road that runs alongside a shady stream before emerging into lush open countryside.

After the grandeur of Angkor's many sites of antiquity, arriving at a relatively modern temple such as Wat Attwiya is to confront the continuity of a centuries-old unbroken Khmer tradition. The temple was founded around 1935 but was completely destroyed by the Khmer Rouge. It was only reconstructed in 1980. Behind the wat are the ruins of a large Angkor-era temple, a tranquil corner to reflect upon the power of Buddhism to triumph over the vicissitudes of a thousand years including some of the horrors of the previous century. About 25 monks live at Wat Attwiya and almost an equal number of acolytes under the age of 21. The canopy of trailing flags in the inner sanctum is said to convey prayers to heaven, carrying the souls of worshippers alongside. But perhaps the great joy of Wat Attwiya is a walk in the ruins: anonymous and rarely visited, they are witness to the rise and ebb of civilizations.

Wat Attwiya liegt idyllisch am Ende einer kurvigen Straße, die entlang eines schattigen Flüsschens verläuft, bevor es sich in der üppigen Vegetation der Landschaft verliert.

Nach dem großartigen Eindruck, den Angkors antike Sehenswürdigkeiten hinterlassen, begegnet man in dem relativ modernen Tempel Wat Attwiya der ungebrochenen Kontinuität der jahrhundertealten Tradition der Khmer. Der 1935 gegründete Tempel wurde von den Roten Khmer bis auf die Grundmauern zerstört und erst 1980 wieder aufgebaut. Hinter dem Wat liegen die Trümmer eines großen Tempels aus der Angkorzeit – ein geeignetes Plätzchen zum Nachdenken über die Kraft des Buddhismus, der über die Gräueltaten von tausend Jahren, insbesondere des letzten Jahrhunderts, triumphiert hat. In Wat Attwiya leben etwa fünfundzwanzig Mönche und fast ebenso viele Novizen unter einundzwanzig Jahren. Die vom Vordach herunterhängenden Gebetsfahnen im zentralen Heiligtum sollen Gebete in den Himmel vermitteln und gleichzeitig die Seelen der Gläubigen mitnehmen. Am meisten jedoch lohnt ein Spaziergang durch die Ruinen von Wat Attwiya, denn sie bezeugen namenlos und unbeachtet das Kommen und Gehen der Kulturen.

C'est au bout d'une route en lacets épousant le cours ombragé d'une rivière que s'élève Vat Attwiya, dans une plaine luxuriante.

Après la magnificence et la profusion des sites antiques d'Angkor, la modernité relative de ce temple s'inscrit dans la continuité de la tradition khmère. Erigé vers 1935, puis complètement détruit par les Khmers rouges, il n'a été reconstruit qu'en 1980. Derrière le vat, on peut voir les ruines d'un grand temple datant de l'époque d'Angkor. Cet endroit paisible invite à réfléchir sur l'aptitude du bouddhisme à triompher des vicissitudes d'un millénaire, et plus particulièrement des tragédies du siècle écoulé. Vat Attwiya est habité par environ 25 moines et un nombre à peu près égal de novices âgés de moins de 21 ans. Les bannières formant une voûte dans le sanctuaire intérieur sont censées emmener les prières et les âmes des fidèles vers les cieux. Mais à Vat Attwiya, il faut se promener dans les ruines : loin des sentiers battus, elles témoignent de la grandeur et du déclin des civilisations.

TAXI
Mr. SUN
Mr. SUN

※ **ABOVE AND RIGHT** Monks in private quarters with their few possessions that include incense, Buddha images and stacks of prayer books. ※ **OBEN UND RECHTE SEITE** In ihren Privaträumen zeigen die Mönche ihre geringen Besitztümer, darunter Räucherstäbchen, Buddhafiguren und stapelweise Gebetbücher. ※ **CI-DESSUS ET À DROITE** Des moines dans leur espace privé avec pour seuls objets personnels de l'encens, des statues du Bouddha et des livres de prière.

※ **PAGES 342–343 CLOCKWISE FROM TOP LEFT** a group of Angkor-period ruins just behind Wat Attwiya. a moped-powered trishaw parked outside the wat. the double-peaked roofs of the wat's meeting hall. The small houses are the monks private quarters. **BELOW** musical instruments, including a traditional xylophone and a pair of drums, in a corner of the meeting hall. **FACING PAGE** The flags hanging above the Buddhas in the main temple are believed to carry prayers as well as the souls of worshippers to heaven. ※ **SEITEN 342–343, IM UHRZEIGERSINN VON LINS OBEN** Diese Ruinen aus der Angkorzeit liegen direkt hinter dem Wat Attwiya. Eine Moped-Trischa parkt vor dem Wat. Der Gemeinschaftsraum der Mönche wurde mit einem zweigiebeligen Dach gekrönt. In den kleineren Häusern leben die Mönche. **UNTEN** Musikinstrumente in einer Ecke des Gemeinschaftsraums, darunter Trommeln und ein traditionelles Xylophon. **RECHTE SEITE** Die Gebetsfahnen über den Buddhafiguren im Haupttempel sollen die Gebete und Seelen der Gläubigen in den Himmel bringen. ※ **PAGES 342–343,DANS LE SENS DES AIGUILLES D'UNE MONTRE, À PARTIER D'EN HAUT GAUCHE** des ruines de l'époque d'Angkor derrière Vat Attwiya. Un *trishaw*, un cyclopousse à moteur, garé devant le vat. La salle commune du vat est surmontée d'un double toit. les petits bâtiments sont les cellules des moires leur espace. **CI-DESSOUS** des instruments de musique, dont un xylophone traditionnel et des tambours dans un coin de la salle commune. **PAGE DE DROITE** Les bannières qui pendent au-dessus des bouddhas du temple principal sont censées emmener aux cieux les prières et les âmes des fidèles.

※ **FACING PAGE** Rows of Buddha images, candles and incense make up a private altar in a monk's chamber. **ABOVE** The meeting hall is decorated with paintings in a simple rustic style, possibly done by different artists at different times. ※ **LINKE SEITE** Zahlreiche Buddhafiguren, Kerzen und Räucherstäbchen bilden in dieser Mönchszelle einen privaten Altar. **OBEN** Die Wände des Gemeinschaftsraums sind mit naiv ländlichen Gemälden verziert, die wahrscheinlich von Künstlern aus verschiedenen Epochen stammen. ※ **PAGE DE GAUCHE** dans la cellule d'un moine, un autel privé avec des bouddhas, des bougies et des bâtonnets d'encens. **CI-DESSUS** La salle commune est ornée de peintures naïves, probablement réalisées par différents artistes au fil du temps.

Nathalie Saphon Ridel
Siem Reap

A reflection on the Buddhist belief of transience.

Nathalie Saphon Ridel's quiet house not far from the temples of Angkor is both an anchorage and an inspiration; it is a reflection of her personal history inexorably tied up with Cambodia's own.

It was built in 1981 at the end of the brutal regime of the Khmer Rouge, when the country was caught in the ravages of civil war. Daughter of a Cambodian father and French mother, Nathalie grew up in Phnom Penh; when the bombings became unbearable the family moved to France. Until Nathalie returned to Cambodia in 1992 she had never visited Siem Reap; after working as a buyer in China for French boutiques, she settled there, drawn by the feeling of impermanence that Buddhist philosophy emphasizes. She started "Khmer Attitude", a design label that produces quality textiles and silver. Together with her husband she expanded the house, adding verandas and guestrooms and replacing partitions with picture windows. In consonance with Nathalie's beliefs, it is simple, pure and reposeful.

Nathalie Saphon Ridels stilles Haus unweit der Tempel von Angkor dient gleichermaßen als Fixpunkt und Inspirationsquelle – spiegelt es doch ihre persönliche Geschichte wider, die mit der Geschichte Kambodschas untrennbar verbunden ist.

Das Haus wurde 1981 erbaut, am Ende der brutalen Herrschaft der Roten Khmer, als das Land in einen blutigen Bürgerkrieg verwickelt war. Nathalie wuchs als Tochter eines kambodschanischen Vaters und einer französischen Mutter in Phnom Penh auf. Als der Bombenterror unerträglich wurde, zog die Familie nach Frankreich. Erst nach ihrer Rückkehr im Jahr 1992 kam Nathalie erstmals nach Siem Reap, wo sie sich in der Folgezeit niederließ. Nachdem sie in China als Einkäuferin für französische Boutiquen gearbeitet hatte, zog sie ein Gefühl der Unbeständigkeit, das auch in der buddhistischen Philosophie eine wesentliche Rolle spielt, in ihr Heimatland zurück. Sie gründete »Khmer Attitude«, ein Designerlabel, unter dem sie hochwertige Textilien und Silberwaren produziert. Gemeinsam mit ihrem Mann erweiterte sie das Haus um Veranden und Gästezimmer, wobei sie die Trennwände durch Panoramafenster ersetzte. Im Einklang mit Nathalies Lebenshaltung ist das Haus schlicht und erholsam.

Située non loin des temples d'Angkor, la paisible demeure de Nathalie Saphon Ridel est à la fois un point d'ancrage et une source d'inspiration. Elle reflète son histoire personnelle, inexorablement liée à celle du Cambodge.

La maison avait été construite en 1981, vers la fin de la dictature sanguinaire des Khmers rouges, alors que la guerre civile faisait rage dans le pays. De père cambodgien et de mère française, Nathalie a grandi à Phnom Penh. Quand les bombardements sont devenus insupportables, la famille s'est réfugiée en France. De retour au Cambodge en 1992, elle s'est installée à Siem Reap, qu'elle visitait pour la première fois, attirée par ce sentiment d'impermanence qui est aussi l'une des vérités enseignées par le bouddhisme. Cette jeune femme, qui avait travaillé comme acheteuse en Chine pour des boutiques françaises, a lancé une marque de textiles de qualité et de bijoux en argent, «Khmer Attitude». Avec le concours de son mari, elle a agrandi la maison en lui ajoutant des vérandas et des chambres d'amis et remplacé les cloisons par des fenêtres panoramiques. En accord avec les croyances de Nathalie, l'endroit est simple, pur et reposant.

※ **FACING PAGE** outside view of the house. earthen floor tiles in the staircase hall. **ABOVE** Nathalie Saphon Ridel with her son Luca. The hammock is made from water hyacinth. The rattan and rubber wood bed is traditional. **FOLLOWING PAGES** A simple mosquito net and paper lamp are typical of the family's spartan style. ※ **LINKE SEITE** Außenansicht des Hauses. Tonfliesen im Treppenhaus. **OBEN** Nathalie Saphon Ridel mit ihrem Sohn Luca. Die Hängematte wurde aus Wasserhyazinthen hergestellt. Das traditionelle Bett ist aus Rattan und dem Holz des Gummibaums gefertigt. **FOLGENDE DOPPELSEITE** Das Schlichtheit des Moskitonetzes und der Papierlampe ist typisch für den spartanischen Einrichtungsstil der Familie. ※ **PAGE DE GAUCHE** la maison dans son environnement naturel. L'escalier débouche sur une pièce au sol carrelé. **CI-DESSUS** Nathalie Saphon Ridel en compagnie de son fils Luca. Le hamac est en fibres de jacinthe d'eau. Le lit en rotin et bois d'hévéa est de facture traditionnelle. **DOUBLE PAGE SUIVANTE** La simple moustiquaire et la lampe en papier caractérisent le style spartiate de cette famille.

Amansara
Siem Reap

The peaceful garden of celestial nymphs.

Step aboard your own private *remork*, the moped-powered trishaw seen opposite, and in ten minutes you are inside Angkor Wat's temple sanctuary.

Amansara has its own fleet of custom-made *remorks*. Set in a garden with an irregular-shaped swimming pool, Amansara's twelve suites are arranged around a grassy courtyard, from which radiate the lounge, library and a dramatic, circular dining space. Built by the French architect Laurent Mondet in 1962 for King Sihanouk to house foreign dignitaries, it once hosted the likes of Charles de Gaulle, Jacqueline Kennedy, Marshall Tito and actor Peter O'Toole, who stayed here while filming "Lord Jim". Following several incarnations, the property was acquired by Amanresorts in 2002 and carefully restored to preserve its Sixties style. The character of the Villa Princiere, as it was known, remains. Amansara derives its names from two Sanskrit words: *Aman* means "peace" and *sara* is taken from *apsara* or "heavenly nymph". So it is the "peaceful garden of celestial nymphs".

Mit einem *remork*, einer Moped-Trischa gelangt man in zehn Minuten von Amansara zu den Tempeln von Angkor.

Das kleine Hotel verfügt über einen eigenen kleinen Fuhrpark dieser eigens angefertigten Fahrzeuge. Die zwölf Suiten liegen in einem Garten mit einem Swimmingpool in ungewöhnlichem Format. Die Suiten gehen auf einen grasbewachsenen Innenhof hinaus, um den sich auch die Lounge, die Bibliothek und ein runder Speiseraum gruppieren. In diesem Bauwerk, das 1962 von dem französischen Architekten Laurent Mondet für König Sihanouk als Gästehaus für ausländische Würdenträger erbaut wurde, waren unter anderem Charles de Gaulle, Jacqueline Kennedy, Marschall Tito und Peter O'Toole zu Gast, letzterer anlässlich der Dreharbeiten zu »Lord Jim«. Nachdem es mehrfach anderweitig genutzt worden war, wurde das Haus schließlich 2002 von der Firma Amanresorts gekauft und sorgfältig restauriert. Der Charakter der Villa Princière, wie das Haus genannt wurde, blieb im Stil der 1960er Jahre erhalten. Der Name Amansara geht auf zwei Sanskritwörter zurück: *Aman* heißt »Frieden«, während *sara* dem Wort Apsara, »weiblicher Geist«, entnommen ist.

Montez dans l'un des nombreux *remork* qu'Amansara tient à la disposition de ses hôtes, et vous serez en dix minutes au cœur du sanctuaire d'Angkor Vat.

Amansara, c'est un jardin doté d'une piscine aux contours irréguliers et 12 suites disposées autour d'une cour gazonnée à partir de laquelle rayonnent un salon, une bibliothèque et un spectaculaire espace circulaire destiné aux repas. Construit par l'architecte français Laurent Mondet en 1962 pour les visiteurs étrangers du roi Norodom Sihanouk, Amansara a accueilli des hôtes de marque tels que le général de Gaulle, Jackie Kennedy, Tito et l'acteur Peter O'Toole, qui y a séjourné pendant le tournage de « Lord Jim ». Après tout un cycle de réincarnations, la propriété a été rachetée en 2002 par Amanresorts, qui l'a rénovée avec soin de manière à préserver son style années 1960 et son caractère de villa princière. Le nom d'Amansara est dérivé des mots sanscrits *aman*, la paix, et *apsara*, nymphe céleste. C'est ainsi que cet hôtel porte le nom poétique de «Jardin paisible des nymphes célestes».

※ **ABOVE** A gardener strolls past a row of bicycles reserved for guests to tour the temples. **BELOW** The lounge is furnished with banquettes and Sixties style furniture. **FACING PAGE** Each suite opens on to an enclosed courtyard with a water garden. **FOLLOWING PAGES** loungers on woven mats by the swimming pool. ※ **OBEN** Ein Gärtner schlendert an den Fahrrädern vorbei, mit denen die Hotelgäste die Tempel erkunden. **UNTEN** Die Lounge ist mit gepolsterten Bänken und Möbeln im Stil der 1960er Jahre eingerichtet. **RECHTE SEITE** An jede Suite schließt sich ein geschlossener Innenhof mit einem Wasserbeckengarten an. **FOLGENDE DOPPELSEITE** Matratzen auf geflochtenen Matten am Swimmingpool. ※ **CI-DESSUS** Un jardinier déambule près des bicyclettes que les clients peuvent emprunter pour visiter les temples. **CI-DESSOUS** Dans le salon, des banquettes et des meubles années 1960 invitent à la détente. **PAGE DE DROITE** Chaque suite donne sur une courette fermée et un jardin d'eau. **DOUBLE PAGE SUIVANTE** des lits de plage posés sur des nattes au bord de la piscine.

ANGKOR
ANGKOR

Bernard Teo
The China Club
OCBC Bank

Singapore

天下為
孫文

THE CHINA CLUB

Singapore

Get shanghaied to the 52nd floor.

High-speed lifts whizz you to a 12,000 square-foot rooftop dining club with 360-degree views of Singapore's skyline and the South China Sea. On a clear day you can see as far as Indonesia and Malaysia.

In dazzling contrast to the long-distance vistas is the atmosphere of a 19th-century Chinese tea room, inspired in equal parts by old Shanghai and Mao memorabilia. Silk lanterns, French wallpaper and swathes of embroidered drapes in the dining room blend with statues and Warhol-inspired images of Chairman Mao in the Long March Bar. Underfoot, the rosewood flooring is stencilled with dragon, butterfly and floral motifs. The blackwood and marble inlaid furniture could have been transported from a warlord's house. Every accessory, from the tin ashtrays to the table china, is emblazoned with Mao's red star. Hong Kong entrepreneur David Tang made the tongue-in-cheek chinoiserie famous when he opened the first of the China Clubs in Hong Kong in 1991. The Singapore club is his latest, irreverent offering.

Der Hochgeschwindigkeitslift bringt Sie hoch aufs Dach in einen 400 m² großen Dining Club mit Rundumsicht auf die Skyline von Singapur und das Südchinesische Meer. Bei gutem Wetter kann man bis nach Indonesien und Malaysia sehen.

Die Aussicht steht in scharfem Kontrast zu der Atmosphäre eines chinesischen Teesalons aus dem 19. Jahrhundert, dessen Einrichtung vom alten Schanghai und Denkwürdigkeiten aus der Zeit Maos inspiriert ist. Seidenlaternen, französische Tapeten und fein bestickte Gardinen im Speisesaal werden mit Statuen und Warhol-inspirierten Bildern des Vorsitzenden Mao in der »Bar des langen Marsches« kombiniert. Der Boden aus Rosenholz ist mit Drachen-, Schmetterlings- und Blumenmustern, die Möbel mit Intarsien aus Palisanderholz und Marmor verziert. Maos roter Stern prangt auf jedem Accessoire vom Blechaschenbecher bis zum Tafelservice. David Tang, ein Unternehmer aus Hongkong, machte diese nicht ganz Ernst gemeinten Adlerhorste berühmt, als er den ersten China Club 1991 in Hongkong eröffnete. Der pietätlose Club in Singapur ist seine jüngste Errungenschaft dieser Art.

Un ascenseur vous emmène à une allure vertigineuse au dernier étage, dans un club-restaurant de 400 m² offrant une vue panoramique sur Singapour et le sud de la mer de Chine.

Quand le ciel est dégagé, vous pouvez apercevoir l'Indonésie et la Malaysia, et cela dans une ambiance de salon de thé chinois du 19e siècle, mêlant le style vieux Shanghai et les souvenirs de Mao. Des lanternes en soie, du papier peint français et des rideaux brodés dans la salle de restaurant se mêlent à des figurines et des représentations de Mao à la Andy Warhol dans le «Bar de la Longue Marche». Sur le plancher en bois de rose, des dragons, des papillons et des motifs floraux ont été peints au pochoir. Le mobilier en marqueterie d'ébène et de marbre semble venir tout droit d'une demeure de seigneur de la guerre. Tous les accessoires, des cendriers en étain à la vaisselle en porcelaine, sont marqués de l'étoile rouge de Mao. David Tang, entrepreneur de Hong-Kong a mis les «chinoiseries» au goût du jour avec l'ouverture de son premier China Club à Hong Kong en 1991. Le club de Singapour est son dernier clin d'œil en date.

※ **FACING PAGE** Borrowed from Mao's army, the club's red star insignia is emblazoned on its china and napery. **ABOVE** French 19th-century wallpaper and flowing swathes of silk in a private dining room. ※ **LINKE SEITE** Der China Club hat den roten Stern der Armee Maos als Insignien ausgeliehen und Service und Tischwäsche damit verziert. **OBEN** Französische Tapeten aus dem 19. Jahrhundert und Seide in verschwenderischem Ausmaß in einem der privaten Speiseräume. ※ **PAGE DE GAUCHE** Emprunt à l'armée de Mao, l'étoile rouge symbole du club apparaît sur la porcelaine et le linge de table. **CI-DESSUS** papier peint français 19ᵉ et drapés de soie dans une salle à manger particulière.

⁂ **FACING PAGE** Gaudy Italian chandeliers and Chinese lattice doors recreate the atmosphere of old Shanghai. **ABOVE** A pagoda-shaped birdcage beside a floor-to-ceiling glass wall overlooking Singapore's skyline. **FOLLOWING PAGES** A youthful portrait of Mao in a Warhol-style silkscreen print. ⁂ **LINKE SEITE** Knallige italienische Kronleuchter und chinesische Spaliertüren beschwören die Atmosphäre des alten Schanghai. **OBEN** ein pagodenförmiger Vogelkäfig neben einem raumhohen Panoramafenster mit Blick auf die Skyline Singapurs. **FOLGENDE DOPPELSEITE** Porträt Maos als junger Mann als Siebdruck im Stile Warhols. ⁂ **PAGE DE GAUCHE** ambiance Vieux Shanghai avec un lustre italien aux couleurs voyantes et des portes à claire-voie chinoises. **CI-DESSUS** une cage à oiseaux en forme de pagode devant une baie vitrée découvrant le panorama de Singapour. **DOUBLE PAGE SUIVANTE** Mao jeune homme, sérigraphie sur soie à la manière de Warhol.

Bernard Teo

Singapore

The Chairman rules in a high-rise apartment.

High up on the fifteenth floor of an early 1960s modernist apartment block in the heart of Singapore, fashion retailer Bernard Teo's flat is a whimsical fusion of the old and new.

The building sits on a hill, overlooking a green belt dotted with pre-war colonial bungalows. Finding it was a pursuit of love: Bernard first saw the flat twenty years ago, when it belonged to a girlfriend, and liked it so much that when it came up for sale six years later, he acquired it and literally took it apart. One of the bedrooms was sacrificed to extend the dining area and, over the years, he has reworked the place to suit his style. Modern art from Bali, industrial lighting saved from hospitals and schools, eclectic furniture and, a rare flowering cactus in an old Javanese copper on the long terrace. Most amusing of all is the 175-piece collection of porcelain figures of Chairman Mao produced during the Cultural Revolution which Bernard started because of his father's uncanny resemblance to the Great Helmsman.

Bernards Teo Wohnung liegt hoch oben im fünfzehnten Stock eines modernistischen Wohnblocks aus den frühen 1960er Jahren mitten in Singapur. Der Boutiquenbesitzer verbindet in der Einrichtung Alt und Neu auf kuriose Weise.

Das Gebäude steht auf einem Hügel, der Blick geht auf einen Grüngürtel mit Bungalows im Kolonialstil. Die Wohnung ging Teo nicht mehr aus dem Kopf, seit er sie vor zwanzig Jahren zum ersten Mal sah. Damals gehörte sie einer Freundin, aber als sie sechs Jahre später zum Verkauf stand, griff er sofort zu. Teo mochte die Wohnung sehr und nahm sie dennoch buchstäblich auseinander. Er opferte ein Schlafzimmer zu Gunsten einer Erweiterung des Esszimmers und gestaltete die Wohnung über die Jahre nach seinem Geschmack um. Eklektizistisch kombinierte er moderne Kunst aus Bali mit Werkslampen, die er aus Schulen oder Krankenhäusern rettete, und diversen Möbelstücken wie dem Wohnzimmersofa im Kolonialstil, das ihm die Bank of China im Zuge einer Renovierung verkaufte. Die kuriose 175 Exemplare umfassende Sammlung von Porzellanfiguren aus der Zeit der Kulturrevolution, die den Großen Vorsitzenden Mao darstellen, begann Bernard Teo wegen der verblüffenden Ähnlichkeit des Politikers mit seinem Vater.

Situé au quinzième étage d'un immeuble construit au début des années 1960 au centre de Singapour, l'appartement de Bernard Teo est un curieux mélange d'ancien et de neuf.

L'immeuble est juché sur une colline, d'où il domine une ceinture verte émaillée de pavillons de style colonial remontant à l'avant-guerre. Son propriétaire est tombé amoureux de l'appartement il y a vingt ans, quand il l'a vu pour la première fois. Il appartenait alors à une de ses amies, et lorsqu'il a été mis en vente six ans plus tard, il en a fait l'acquisition parce qu'il l'aimait toujours autant – ce qui ne l'a pas empêché de le mettre littéralement en pièces. Il a sacrifié une des chambres pour agrandir le coin repas et, au fil des ans, il a remodelé le logement à son goût. De l'art moderne balinais et des éclairages industriels récupérés dans des hôpitaux ou des écoles côtoient des meubles hétéroclites. Le plus amusant de la décoration est la collection de 175 présidents Mao en porcelaine produits pendant la Révolution culturelle, collection que Bernard Teo avait commencée à cause de la troublante ressemblance entre son père et le Grand Timonier …

⁂ **PREVIOUS PAGE** Terrace doors open to frame the city's skyline. **FACING PAGES AND ABOVE** A cabinet of curiosities is filled with Bernard Teo's collection of porcelain Mao figures which overflow into the sofa's niche. ⁂ **VORHERGEHENDE DOPPELSEITE** Durch die Balkontür geht der Blick auf die Skyline der Stadt. **LINKE SEITE UND OBEN** Das Kuriositätenkabinett enthält Bernard Teos Sammlung von Porzellanfiguren Maos, die bis in die Sofaecke vordringen. ⁂ **DOUBLE PAGE PRECEDENTE** Les portes de la terrasse encadrent la vue de la ville avec ses gratte-ciel. **PAGE DE GAUCHE ET CI-DESSUS ET DOUBLE PAGE SUIVANTE** A l'étroit dans un cabinet de curiosités, la collection de Mao en porcelaine de Bernard Teo se déverse dans la niche aménagée pour le sofa.

※ **ABOVE** The colonial-style sofa was thrown out by the Bank of China when they were renovating their office. **BELOW** A painting titled "Positive Negative" by Balinese artist Taman hangs above a 1940s Art Deco dining table. **FACING PAGE** In the living area Jasper Morrison chairs by Capellini and a sofa are arranged around an old Indian table. ※ **OBEN** Die Bank of China entledigte sich im Laufe einer Renovierung dieses Sofas im Kolonialstil. **UNTEN** Hinter dem Art-déco-Esstisch aus den 1940er Jahren hängt das Bild »Positive Negative« des balinesischen Malers Taman. **RECHTE SEITE** Im Wohnbereich stehen ein Sofa und Jasper-Morrison-Stühle von Capellini um einen alten indischen Tisch. ※ **CI-DESSUS** La Bank of China avait mis au rebut ce canapé de style colonial à l'occasion d'une rénovation. **CI-DESSOUS** Une œuvre de l'artiste balinais Taman intitulée *Positive Negative* est accrochée au-dessus d'une table Art déco des années 1940. **PAGE DE DROITE** Dans le séjour, un canapé et des chaises de Jasper Morrison fabriquées par Capellini sont disposés autour d'une table indienne ancienne.

※ **ABOVE** Photographs of Tibetan children by American photo journalist Phil Borges hang above an Art-Deco style cabinet. **FACING PAGE** In the bedroom an African chair with sensuous lines lends interest. The painting on the wall is a self-portrait by Balinese artist Made Djirna. ※ **OBEN** Die Fotos von tibetischen Kindern des amerikanischen Bildjournalisten Phil Borges hängen über einer Vitrine im Art-déco-Stil. **RECHTE SEITE** Der sinnlich anmutende afrikanische Stuhl steht im Schlafzimmer. An der Wand hängt ein Selbstporträt des balinesischen Künstlers Made Djirna. ※ **CI-DESSUS** Au-dessus d'un meuble bas Art déco, photographies d'enfants tibétains prises par le photo-journaliste Phil Borges. **PAGE DE DROITE** Une chaise africaine aux lignes sensuelles donne un petit quelque chose à la chambre. Le tableau au mur est un autoportrait de l'artiste balinais Made Djirna.

A HOUSE BY THE RESERVOIR

SINGAPORE

Living in a modern water pavilion.

The house by the reservoir was commissioned by a businessman who finds many of the conventions of minimalism in modern architecture repetitive and predictable. Such houses often end up looking the same, a style he calls "straight-lined tropical".

For the owner, the first achievement of his recently finished home was the plot's idyllic location near MacRitchie Reservoir, a green lung in the bustling commercial metropolis. The reservoir and its catchment area in fact became the inspired metaphor for the house. Architect Soo K. Chan extended the sense of greenery and water by providing two swimming pools, one of them infinity-edged, the overflow from which forms a running channel. The water bodies are flanked by granite walls skillfully built from stone blocks of varying sizes; like sculptural reliefs they break the monotony of line and surface. Double volume plate glass windows and an open-air atrium give the three wings of the house a well-proportioned lightness. Singapore's old reservoir has acquired a water pavilion in its vicinity.

Das kürzlich erst fertig gestellte Haus wurde von einem Geschäftsmann in Auftrag gegeben, der viele Elemente des Minimalismus in der modernen Architektur eintönig und vorhersehbar findet. Solche Häuser ähneln sich oft in einem Stil, den er »gradlinig tropisch« nennt.

Für ihn selbst fing alles damit an, dass er das idyllische Grundstück in der Nähe des MacRitchie-Reservoirs fand, einer grünen Lunge in der geschäftigen Handelsmetropole. Das Wasserreservoir und das angrenzende Sammelgebiet entwickelten sich zum Leitmotiv für das Haus. Der Architekt Soo K. Chan weitete die Vorstellung von Wasser und Grün aus und ließ zwei Swimmingpools bauen – der eine läuft an einem Ende stets über und strömt in einen fließenden Kanal. Um die Wasserbecken stehen Granitmauern, die geschickt aus unterschiedlich großen Steinblöcken gefertigt wurden. Wie die Reliefs eines Bildhauers brechen sie die Eintönigkeit der Begrenzungen und Oberflächen. Doppelglasfenster und ein Open-Air-Atrium verleihen den drei Flügeln des Hauses eine wohlproportionierte Leichtigkeit. Neben dem alten Wasserspeicher von Singapur steht jetzt ein Pavillon am Wasser.

Cette maison récemment achevée a été commandée par un homme d'affaires qui trouve que nombre des conventions du minimalisme en architecture moderne sont répétitives et prévisibles. Les maisons finissent toujours par être dans ce style qu'il appelle « tropical constant ».

Pour le propriétaire, c'est la situation idyllique du terrain à proximité du MacRitchie Reservoir, un poumon vert dans la trépidante métropole commerçante, qui se trouve à l'origine du projet. La maison reprend la métaphore du réservoir et de son bassin hydrologique. Développant les thèmes de la verdure et de l'eau, l'architecte Soo K. Chan a prévu deux piscines, dont l'une s'écoule à l'infini : son trop-plein se déverse dans une rigole. Les pièces d'eau sont flanquées de murs habilement montés à partir de blocs de granite de différentes tailles, tels des reliefs rompant la monotonie de la ligne et de la surface. Des baies vitrées en double épaisseur et un atrium à ciel ouvert confèrent une légèreté équilibrée aux trois ailes de la maison. Le réservoir historique de Singapour a désormais son pavillon d'eau.

※ **PREVIOUS PAGES** A sense of water suffuses the courtyards of the house. A waterfall in the channel that runs along the house. The main bathroom gives on to an open-air shower area. **BELOW** View from the pool looking towards the pavilion. **FACING PAGE** A cantilevered staircase with a glass and steel balustrade links the living area to the private rooms above. **FOLLOWING PAGES** Comfortable streamlined furniture adorns the rooms that open on to views of water bodies and garden terraces. ※ **VORHERGEHENDE DOPPELSEITE** Die Innenhöfe des Hauses sind von der Sinnlichkeit des Wassers erfüllt. Ein Wasserfall ergießt sich in den kleinen Kanal des Hauses. An das große Bazimmer ist auch eine Außendusche angecshlossen. **UNTEN** Blick vom Swimmingpool zum Pavillon. **RECHTE SEITE** Die freitragende Treppe mit einem Geländer aus Stahl und Glas führt vom Wohnbereich nach oben zu den Privatgemächern. **FOLGENDE DOPPELSEITE** bequeme stromlinienförmige Möblierung der Räume, die auf das Wasser und die terrassenförmig angelegten Gärten hinausgehen. ※ **DOUBLE PAGE PRÉCÉDENTE** L'eau est très présente dans les cours intérieures. chute d'eau dans la rigole qui fait le tour de la mainson. La salle de bain principale donne sur une douche en plein air. **CI-DESSOUS** De la piscine on voit très bien le pavillon. **PAGE DE DROITE** Un escalier suspendu doté d'un garde-corps en verre et acier fait le lien entre le séjour et les pièces privées à l'étage. **DOUBLE PAGE SUIVANTE** Mobilier aux lignes épurées dans les pièces donnant sur les bassins et les jardins en terrasse.

C.C. LOO

Singapore

The classical spirit of a Chinese garden.

To preserve the stylish elegance of Singapore's Belmont Road residential district, the government decreed that each house must be built on a minimum plot size of 1500 sq. meters.

C. C. Loo, a barrister and third-generation Singaporean of Chinese origin, and his wife Sonia set their heart on a modern house that would somehow capture the essence of a classical Chinese garden. Commissioning the well-known architect Mok Wei Wei, they got a home that surpassed their expectations: a place of airy lightness and double volumes in which the slender supporting columns echo the stands of bamboo in the rock garden and indoor spaces evoke the feeling of Chinese water pavilions. Although many of the features – concrete, plate glass and a swimming pool – are modern, the house is built around traditional courtyards, pebbled paths and a pond filled with 99 koi. C. C. and Sonia Loo's contemporary home evokes an ancient spirit and is shared by their young son and a German Shepherd called July.

Per Gesetz will die Regierung die edle Eleganz des Wohngebiets um die Belmont Road bewahren. Demnach dürfen neue Häuser nur auf einer Grundfläche von mindestens 1500 m² errichtet werden.

C. C. Loo, ein Anwalt chinesischer Abstammung, dessen Familie mittlerweile in der dritten Generation in Singapur ansässig ist, und seine Frau Sonia wünschten sich ein modernes Haus mit dem meditativen Charakter eines klassischen chinesischen Gartens. Sie beauftragten den bekannten Architekten Mok Wei Wei, dessen Entwurf ihre kühnsten Erwartungen übertraf. Ihr Haus zeichnet sich durch luftige Leichtigkeit und sehr hohe Räume aus, deren schlanke Stützpfeiler die Form der Bambusstauden im Steingarten wieder aufnehmen, während die Anordnung der Zimmer eine Vision chinesischer Wasserpavillons heraufbeschwört. Obwohl das Haus viele moderne Merkmale aufweist – Beton, Tafelglas und einen Swimmingpool –, ist es um traditionelle Innenhöfe, Kieswege und einen Teich mit 99 Koi herumgebaut. C. C. und Sonia Loo bewohnen das zeitgenössische Haus, das eine jahrhundertealte Spiritualität ausstrahlt, mit ihrem Sohn und der Schäferhündin July.

Afin de préserver l'élégance raffinée du quartier résidentiel de Belmont Road, le gouvernement a décrété que chaque maison devait être construite sur une parcelle d'au minimum 1500 m².

C.C. Loo, avocat et Singapourien de troisième génération d'origine chinoise, et son épouse Sonia voulaient à tout prix une maison moderne qui capte l'essence des jardins chinois classiques. Le célèbre architecte Mok Wei Wei leur a créé un chez-soi dépassant leurs espérances : un lieu de vie clair et spacieux, très haut de plafond, dont les graciles colonnes porteuses font écho aux bosquets de bambous dans le jardin de pierre, et dont les espaces intérieurs rappellent l'ambiance des pavillons d'eau chinois. Malgré la prépondérance d'éléments modernes – béton, vitrages et piscine –, la maison est construite autour de cours traditionnelles, de sentiers recouverts de galets et d'un bassin dans lequel évoluent 99 carpes koi. Aussi l'appartement de style contemporain de Sonia Loo est-il habité par l'esprit des temps passés. Les époux Loo y vivent avec leur jeune fils et leur berger allemand July.

※ **ABOVE** view from the garden of the elevation of the house. The bridge links the study to the dining room. **BELOW** Two Ming dynasty mandarins carved in wood guard the long corridor dining room. **FACING PAGE** Vertical windows overlook the koi pond afloat with water lilies. ※ **OBEN** Blick vom Garten auf das Haus. Die Brücke verbindet das Arbeitszimmer mit dem Esszimmer. **UNTEN** Die beiden holzgeschnitzten Mandarine aus der Ming-Dynastie bewachen den langen Korridor, in dem auch gegessen wird. **RECHTE SEITE** Hohe schmale Fenster gehen auf den mit Seerosen geschmückten Koi-Teich hinaus. ※ **CI-DESSUS** la façade de la maison vue du jardin. Le pont relie le bureau à la salle à manger. **CI-DESSOUS** Deux mandarins Ming sculptés sur bois veillent sur la longue salle à manger-couloir. **PAGE DE DROITE** De hautes fenêtres étroites donnent sur le bassin recouvert de nénuphars où s'ébattent les carpes koi.

※ **FACING PAGE** Pebbles and mosaic tiles line the path from the swimming pool to the garden. The view between two overlapping Chinese-style granite walls is of the swimming pool and the dining room. **ABOVE AND FOLLOWING PAGES** Ming dynasty chairs in the dining room are framed by views of bamboo in the rock garden. On the marble coffee table are two pieces of bronze sculpture by a contemporary Singapore artist. ※ **LINKE SEITE** Der Weg vom Swimmingpool in den Garten ist mit Kies und Mosaik ausgelegt. Durch die beiden versetzt stehenden Granitmauern in chinesischem Stil sieht man den Swimmingpool und das Esszimmer. **OBEN UND FOLGENDE DOPPELSEITE** Stühle aus der Ming-Dynastie im Esszimmer in Kombination mit Bambusstauden im Steingarten. Auf dem marmornen Couchtisch liegen zwei Bronzeskulpturen eines zeitgenössischen Singapurer Künstlers. ※ **PAGE DE GAUCHE** Un chemin de galets et de mosaïque relie la piscine au jardin. Entre deux murs en granite de style chinois, on peut contempler la piscine et la salle à manger. **CI-DESSUS ET DOUBLE PAGE SUIVANTE** Dans la salle à manger, des chaises Ming se détachent sur un fond de bambous. Les deux bronzes posés sur la table basse en marbre, sont l'œuvre d'un artiste local contemporain.

The House of Two Doctors Singapore

Serenity and space in a bamboo grove.

Dr. Tong Ming Chuan is one of Singapore's leading cardiothoracic surgeons. His wife Dr. Geh Min is an eye surgeon. They wanted a house that was a peaceful counterpoint to their busy, often stressful professional lives – a timeless classic of understated, contemporary elegance.

They approached the redoubtable Singapore-based architectural practice of Kerry Hill to design a family home around garden terraces and water bodies that would also house their fine collection of Chinese furniture, calligraphy and Sung porcelain. The two doctors dislike excessive ornamentation; music plays an important part in their lives. Kerry Hill's use of natural materials – slate roof, wooden shutters and limestone floors – and wide eaves and high ceilings keeps the house naturally cool. Much of the house is screened by delicate timber lattices that can be operated to modulate light. In some parts the screens are left open for cross ventilation. The play of light, water, sky and garden creates a unified space of intimacy and contemplation.

Dr. Tong Ming Chuan ist einer der besten Herz-Lungen-Chirurgen in Singapur, während seine Frau Dr. Geh Min als Augenchirurgin arbeitet. Die beiden sehnten sich nach einem Haus, das einen friedlichen Kontrapunkt zu ihrem geschäftigen, stressigen Berufsleben bilden sollte – zeitlos klassisch sowie zurückhaltend, aber zeitgenössisch elegant.

Sie gaben dem in Singapur ansässigen renommierten Architekturbüro Kerry Hills den Auftrag, ein Familienhaus um bepflanzte Terrassen und Wasserbecken herum zu bauen, das genügend Platz für ihre ausgesuchte Sammlung chinesischer Möbel, von Kalligrafien und Sung-Porzellan bieten sollte. Die beiden Ärzte können überschwängliche Dekoration nicht leiden; Musik dagegen spielt eine große Rolle in ihrem Leben. Kerry Hill entschied sich für natürliche Baumaterialien – Schieferdach, hölzerne Fensterläden und Kalksteinböden – sowie herausragende Dachvorsprünge und hohe Decken, damit das Haus auf natürliche Weise kühl bleibt. Das Haus ist weitgehend mit feinen hölzernen Spalieren ausgestattet, mit deren Hilfe man die Menge des Lichteinfalls bestimmen kann. An einigen Stellen bleiben die Spaliere zum Querlüften offen. Die verspielte Zusammenwirkung von Licht, Wasser, Himmel und Gärten schafft einen intimen kontemplativen Raum.

Tong Ming Chuan, l'un des plus grands spécialistes de chirurgie cardio-thoracique, et son épouse Geh Min, spécialisée en chirurgie ophtalmique, ont une vie professionnelle chargée et souvent stressante. Aussi voulaient-ils une maison qui soit un havre de paix, un classique intemporel d'élégance contemporaine discrète.

C'est ainsi qu'ils ont commandé au redoutable cabinet d'architecture singapourien de Kerry Hill une maison organisée autour de terrasses-jardins et de bassins d'eau et qui soit susceptible d'accueillir leur superbe collection de meubles chinois, de calligraphie et de porcelaine Song. Ce couple de chirurgiens n'aime pas la décoration trop chargée et accorde une place importante à la musique dans sa vie. Les matériaux naturels – ardoise pour la toiture, bois pour les volets et calcaire pour les sols – les avant-toits profonds et la belle hauteur sous plafond maintiennent de manière naturelle une certaine fraîcheur dans la maison. La plupart des baies vitrées sont doublées de délicats panneaux en bois à lamelles orientables pour moduler l'éclairage. Certains de ces panneaux sont ouverts de façon à faire courant d'air. Le jeu de la lumière, de l'eau, du ciel et du jardin crée un espace harmonieux d'intimité et de contemplation.

⁂ **FACING PAGE** Entrance lattice doors overlook the reflecting pool. **ABOVE** reading corner with Chinese reclining chairs. **BELOW** living room with a raised music area. **FOLLOWING PAGES** cello and Chinese drum stool in the study. Pomegranates and lotus pods in a lacquer dish. ⁂ **LINKE SEITE** Durch die Holzgittertüren erspäht man den Swimmingpool. **OBEN** Leseecke mit Ruhesesseln. **UNTEN** Wohnzimmer mit Podium zum Musizieren. **FOLGENDE DOPPELSEITE** Cello und chinesischer Schlagzeughocker im Arbeitszimmer. Granatäpfel und Lotushülsen in einer Lackschale. ⁂ **PAGE DE GAUCHE** La porte à claire-voie donne sur la piscine aux eaux miroitantes. **CI-DESSUS** un coin lecture équipé de chaises chinoises à dossier inclinable. **CI-DESSOUS** le salon avec son coin musique sur une estrade. **DOUBLE PAGE SUIVANTE** violoncelle et tabouret de batteur chinois dans le bureau. Des grenades et des cosses de lotus sont disposées dans une coupe en laque.

SCALES – FOUR OCTAVES
C major
C melodic minor
C harmonic minor

※ **FACING PAGE** The terraced pool links two parts of the house. Willow branches frame the patio. **ABOVE** The pavilion overlooking the jade green swimming pool is screened by traveller's palms. ※ **LINKE SEITE** Der terrassenförmig angelegte Swimmingpool verbindet zwei Seiten des Hauses. Weidenzweige rahmen den Patio ein. **OBEN** Der Pavillon am Rand des jadegrünen Swimmingpools wird von Palmen abgeschirmt. ※ **PAGE DE GAUCHE** La piscine en terrasse relie les deux parties de la maison. un patio à l'ombre d'un saule. **CI-DESSUS** Le pavillon donnant sur la piscine vert jade est protégé des regards par un écran de palmiers.

The Blue Mansion
House on Heeren Street

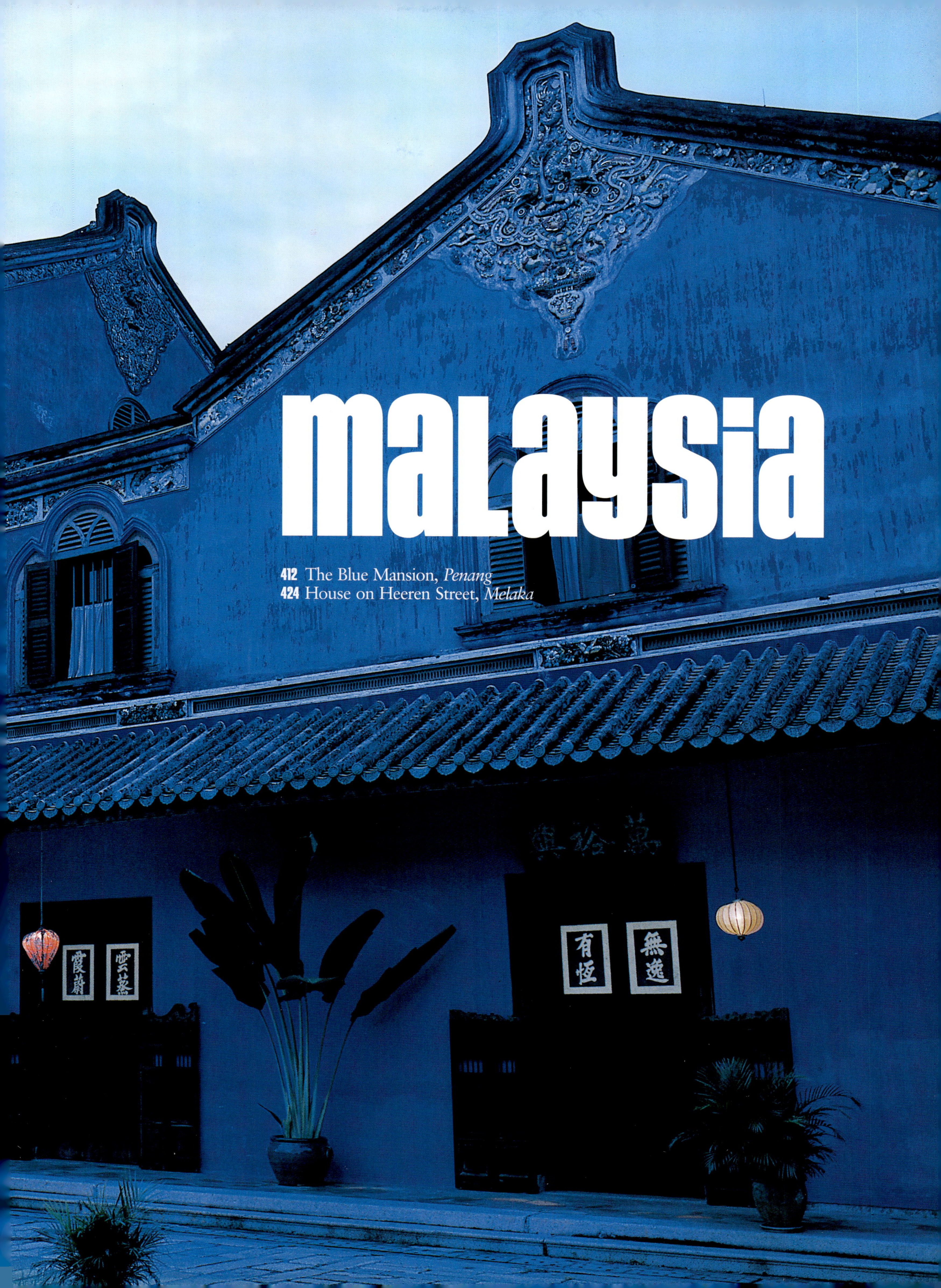

MALAYSIA

雲蒸
霞蔚

The Blue Mansion
Penang

A deep blue embrace.

Two remarkable people gave the Blue Mansion its life and afterlife in historic Georgetown on the island of Penang. It was built by Cheong Fatt Tze, a late 19th-century Chinese merchant so wealthy he was called the "Rockefeller of the East".

And architect Laurence Loh, who acquired the decaying mansion in 1990, spent a decade restoring it with his wife Lin Lee Loh-Lim. Cheong Fatt Tze owned other homes, in Singapore, Hong Kong and China, but he lavished riches on his showpiece, importing wrought-iron pillars and balcony grilles from Glasgow and shiploads of floor tiles from Stoke-on-Trent. Putting life back into the indigo-painted courtyard house became the Lohs' mission. Their attentions have been no less lavish. Craftsmen were brought in from China to recreate porcelain mosaic decoration on the façade and every artifact, including a magnificent carved and gilded screen, is an authentic period piece. The award-winning conversion of the Blue Mansion into a 16-room boutique hotel is so impressive that it made a star appearance in the film "Indochine" with Catherine Deneuve.

Das Blue Mansion im historischen Georgetown auf der Insel Penang verdankt seine Existenz und seinen Ruf zwei bemerkenswerten Persönlichkeiten. Gebaut hat es Cheong Fatt Tze, ein Kaufmann des späten 19. Jahrhunderts, der so reich war, dass er als »Rockefeller des Ostens« galt.

Restauriert wurde es von dem Architekten Laurence Loh, der das Herrenhaus 1990 kaufte und in den folgenden Jahren mit seiner Frau von Grund auf renovierte. Cheong Fatt Tze besaß Häuser in Singapur, Hongkong und China, doch vor allem sein Paradestück ließ er prunkvoll ausstatten – mit aus Glasgow importierten schmiedeeisernen Säulen und Balkongittern und Fliesen aus Stoke-on-Trent. Dem blau getünchten, um einen Innenhof herum gebauten Haus neues Leben einzuhauchen, betrachteten die Lohs als ihre Mission und scheuten dafür weder Mühe noch Geld. Handwerker wurden aus China eingeflogen, um die Mosaikverzierung aus Porzellan an der Fassade wiederherzustellen. Überdies stammt jedes Artefakt, darunter die herrliche holzgeschnitzte vergoldete Trennwand, aus dem 19. Jahrhundert. Die preisgekrönte Verwandlung des Blue Mansion in ein Hotel mit sechzehn Zimmern ist so überzeugend, dass es neben Catherine Deneuve eine Hauptrolle in dem Film »Indochina« spielen durfte.

Un couple remarquable a ramené la Villa bleue à la vie. Située dans la ville historique de Georgetown, sur l'île de Pinang, elle avait été construite à la fin du 19e siècle par Cheong Fatt Tze, dit le « Rockefeller de l'Orient ».

L'architecte Laurence Loh, qui a fait l'acquisition en 1990 de cette maison tombant en ruine, a mis une dizaine d'années à la restaurer, secondé dans cette tâche par son épouse Lin Lee Loh-Lim. Cheong Fatt Tze possédait plusieurs autres maisons, à Singapour, Hong-Kong et en Chine, mais c'est la Villa bleue qui avait sa préférence. Il n'a pas regardé à la dépense, important de Glasgow des colonnes et balustrades en fer forgé et de Stoke-on-Trent de pleines cargaisons de carreaux de faïence. Considérant que leur mission était de redonner vie à cette maison à patio, les Loh n'ont pas non plus ménagé leurs efforts. Ils ont fait venir de Chine des artisans qui ont reconstitué le décor en mosaïque de la façade, et ils ont veillé à ce que le moindre objet, dont un magnifique paravent en bois sculpté et doré à l'or fin, soit une authentique pièce d'époque. La transformation, primée par l'Unesco, de la Villa bleue en un hôtel proposant 16 suites à prix doux est si convaincante que la villa a servi de décor au tournage d'« Indochine » avec Catherine Deneuve.

FACING PAGE Louvred windows, typical of Penang's period architecture, line the corridors on the upper floor. The film crew of "Indochine" left three old rickshaws standing in the front. The shaded arcade is hung with Chinese lanterns and lined with floor tiles originally imported from Britain. **ABOVE** The mansion's indigo limewashed front elevation is set with shuttered Gothic windows, a sheltered walkway and double-layered timber doors. ❊ **LINKE SEITE** Die Jalousienfenster, die reihenweise auf die oberen Flure hinausgehen, sind charakteristisch für Penang im 19. Jahrhundert. Die »Indochina«-Filmcrew ließ drei alte Rikschas vor dem Haus zurück. Der schattige Bogengang ist mit chinesischen Laternen und Bodenfliesen aus England geschmückt. **OBEN** die Stirnansicht in blauem Kalkanstrich, mit gotischen Fenstern und Fensterläden, einem überdachten Gang und zweiflügeligen Holztüren. ❊ **PAGE DE GAUCHE** Les couloirs du premier étage sont bordés de fenêtres à claire-voie, éléments caractéristiques de l'architecture de la période de Penang. Ces trois rickshaws de collection ont été laissés sur place par l'équipe du tournage d'« Indochine ». Des lanternes chinoises et des carreaux de faïence importés d'Angleterre agrémentent l'arcade ombragée. Le carrelage est d'origine. **CI-DESSUS** La façade avant peinte à la chaux teinte à l'indigo est rythmée par des fenêtres gothiques fermées par des volets, un avant-toit sur toute sa longueur et des portes en bois à deux vantaux doubles.

FACING PAGE AND ABOVE The central courtyard is lined with painted wrought-iron pillars and balcony grilles made by the Victorian firm of MacFarlanes in Glasgow, Scotland. The open space acts as well for circulating air in the house. The louvred windows on the upper floor can be manoeuvred to modulate light. **BELOW** An antique bench at the base of one of the seven staircases. ❊ **LINKE SEITE UND OBEN** Den zentralen Innenhof zieren bemalte schmiedeeiserne Säulen, die ebenso wie die Balkongitter von MacFarlanes, einem viktorianischen Betrieb im schottischen Glasgow, angefertigt wurden. Der große, hohe Innenhof sorgt für Lüftung im Haus. An den Jalousienfenstern im zweiten Stockwerk kann man den Lichteinfall einstellen. **UNTEN** Eine antike Bank am Aufgang einer der sieben Treppen. ❊ **PAGE DE GAUCHE ET CI-DESSUS** La cour intérieure est bordée de colonnes et de balustrades en fer forgé peint, fabriquées à l'époque victorienne par l'entreprise écossaise MacFarlanes à Glasgow. Cet espace ouvert sert aussi à la circulation de l'air dans la maison. Il est possible de moduler la lumière filtrant par les fenêtres à claire-voie du premier étage. **CI-DESSOUS** Un banc ancien au pied de l'un des sept escaliers de la maison.

FACING PAGE Panels of filigreed wood carving are fitted above the wrought-iron grille-work of the balcony. A magnificent carved and gilded floor-to-ceiling screen divides the courtyard from the entrance hall. **ABOVE** Breakfast is served along one side of the central courtyard. ❊ **LINKE SEITE** Über dem schmiedeeisernen Balkongitter ist eine filigran geschnitzte Holzvertäfelung angebracht. Eine prächtig geschnitzte und vergoldete Trennwand, die vom Boden bis zur Decke reicht, trennt den Innenhof von der Eingangshalle. **OBEN** An der einen Seite des zentralen Innenhofs wird das Frühstück serviert. ❊ **PAGE DE GAUCHE** Des panneaux de bois finement sculptés font pendant aux éléments en fer forgé du balcon. Un magnifique claustra sculpté et doré sépare la cour intérieure du hall d'entrée. **CI-DESSUS** On sert le petit-déjeuner sous une des arcades de la cour centrale.

PREVIOUS PAGES a decorative wood screen in a suite. Each carved panel was gilded with gold leaf and protected with organic shellac. **ABOVE AND FACING PAGE** All 16 themed bedrooms are individually furnished with authentic period furniture, and named: the bedroom is called "Peony" right. ❊ **VORHERGEHENDE DOPPELSEITE** eine dekorative Trennwand aus Holz im Wohnbereich der Suite. die Elemente der geschnitzten Holzvertäfelung wurde mit Blattgold überzogen und mit Schellack versiegelt. **OBEN UND RECHTE SEITE** 16 thematisch gestaltete Hotelzimmer wurden mit historischen Möbeln eingerichtet: das Zimmer rechts heisst »Pfingstrose«. ❊ **DOUBLE PAGE PRECEDENTE** un claustra décoratif. Les panneaux sculptés ont été dorés à la feuille d'or et enduits de laque naturelle. **CI-DESSUS ET PAGE DE DROIT** Chaque chambre a une décoration, avec des meubles d'époque, et son nom: La chambre à droite porte le nom « Pivoine ».

House on Heeren Street Melaka

Past preserved in contemplation.

Situated on the Malaysian peninsula with the island of Sumatra just across the narrow Strait of Melaka, the heyday of the town, once known as Malacca, began in the 15th century as a vital trading port on the spice route between India and China.

For about 300 years the Portuguese, Dutch and the British jockeyed for control of this strategic entrepot. By the early 20th century, though, what remained of Melaka was its layered history, a palimpsest of European, Chinese and Malay influences. Singapore-based architect Soo K. Chan was commissioned to resurrect a dilapidated pre-war building, a pastiche of Melaka's eclectic baroque style, as a meditative retreat by a client in Hong Kong. The idea was to preserve the building's atmosphere but prevent further structural decay and make it safe for occupancy. Soo Chan's solutions were minimal and spare: a series of steel frames to support the linked courtyards and a black reflecting pool to heighten its air of a lost oasis regained.

Die Stadt auf der Malaiischen Halbinsel, von der Insel Sumatra nur durch die enge Melakastraße getrennt, war im 15. Jahrhundert unter dem Namen Melaka als lebhafter Handelshafen auf der Gewürzroute zwischen Indien und China weltbekannt.

Portugiesen, Holländer und Briten wechselten sich 300 Jahre lang als Kolonialherren in diesem strategischen Handelshafen ab. Im frühen 20. Jahrhundert war von Melaka jedoch nur die vielschichtige Historie geblieben – ein Palimpsest europäischer, chinesischer und malaiischer Einflüsse. Soo K. Chan, ein Architekt aus Singapur, erhielt von einem Kunden aus Hongkong den Auftrag, ein baufälliges Gebäude in Melakas eklektizistischem Barockstil aus der Zeit vor dem Krieg in einen zur Meditation einladenden Zufluchtsort umzubauen. Der weitere Verfall sollte verhindert und das Haus in einen bewohnbaren Zustand versetzt werden, ohne die ursprüngliche Atmosphäre zu zerstören. In diesem Sinne beschränkte sich Soo Chan auf wenige sparsame Eingriffe: Stahlträger stützen nun die miteinander verbundenen Innenhöfe, und ein schwarzer Swimmingpool betont den Eindruck einer wiedergewonnenen Oase.

Située sur la péninsule malaise, qui n'est séparée de l'île de Sumatra que par le détroit de Malacca, cette ville, connue autrefois sous le nom de Malacca, a pris son essor au 15e siècle. C'était alors un comptoir florissant sur la route des épices reliant l'Inde à la Chine.

Pendant près de trois siècles, Portugais, Hollandais et Britanniques se sont disputés le contrôle de cet entrepôt stratégique. Cependant, ce qui restait de Melaka au début du 20e siècle était une histoire marquée successivement par les influences européenne, chinoise et malaise, comme un palimpseste. Un client de Hong-Kong a chargé l'architecte singapourien Soo K. Chan de relever de ses ruines un bâtiment datant de l'avant-guerre, pastiche du style éclectique baroque de la ville, et de le transformer en un refuge propice à la méditation. L'idée de départ était de préserver l'aura de l'édifice, tout en empêchant de nouvelles dégradations majeures et en assurant la sécurité de ses occupants. Soo K. Chan a donné dans le minimalisme et la sobriété : des profils métalliques assurent la stabilité du réseau de cours intérieures, et un bassin d'un noir réfléchissant la lumière accentue l'apparence d'oasis que la maison a retrouvée.

PREVIOUS PAGE The pebbled bamboo court lead to the living area. **FACING PAGE** The bench and swing were made from old timbers found on the site. **ABOVE** Wooden lattices frame as well as screen views of the bamboo garden. ❊ **RIGHT** The sleeping area inside the wooden screen is set apart from the old walls. **FOLLOWING PAGES** The sleeping area is supported by steel frames by the pool. The existing walls have been left to weather naturally. ❊ **VORHERGEHENDE DOPPELSEITE** der mit Bambuspflanzen und Kies geschmückte Eingangshof. **LINKE SEITE** Bank und Schaukel wurden aus alten herumliegenden Balken hergestellt. **OBEN** Durch das hölzerne Gitterwerk und die Trennwände blickt man in den Bambusgarten. **RECHTS** Das Schlafgemach innerhalb der hölzernen Trennwände wurde abseits der alten Mauern eingerichtet. **FOLGENDE DOPPELSEITE** Der Schlafbereich wird von den Stahlträgern am Swimmingpool gehalten. Die bestehenden Mauern wurden der natürlichen Verwitterung überlassen. ❊ **DOUBLE PAGE PRECEDENTE** La cour est couverte de galets et plantée de bambous. **PAGE DE GAUCHE** Le banc et la balançoire sont en bois de récupération. **CI-DESSUS** On aperçoit le jardin de bambou à travers les persiennes en bois. **A DROITE** L'espace couchage enfermé dans un caisson à lattes forme une unité distincte. **DOUBLE PAGE SUIVANTE** L'espace couchage à l'aplomb de la piscine repose sur des poutrelles métalliques. Les murs d'origine sont abandonnés aux outrages du temps.

IMPRINT

To stay informed about upcoming TASCHEN titles, please request our magazine at www.taschen.com/magazine or write to TASCHEN, Hohenzollernring 53, D–50672 Cologne, Germany, contact@taschen.com, Fax: +49-221-254919. We will be happy to send you a free copy of our magazine which is filled with information about all of our books.

Hohenzollernring 53
D-50672 Köln
www.taschen.com

CONCEPT, EDITING AND LAYOUT BY
Angelika Taschen, Berlin

DESIGN
Sense/Net, Andy Disl and Birgit Reber, Cologne

GENERAL PROJECT MANAGEMENT
Stephanie Bischoff, Cologne

TEXT COORDINATION AND EDITING
Kirsten E. Lehmann, Cologne

GERMAN TRANSLATION
Anne Brauner, Cologne

FRENCH TRANSLATION
Christèle Jany, Cologne

LITHOGRAPHY MANAGEMENT
Horst Neuzner, Cologne

LITHOGRAPHY
lithotronic media gmbh, Frankfurt am Main

COVER
Drawings of the Garudas by Robert Beer, Oxford

Printed in Italy
ISBN: 978-3-8228-4818-0